Watch This!

Cycle C Sermons for Pentecost Day through
Proper 17 / Ordinary Time 22 / Pentecost 12
Based on the Gospel Texts

Dave Zuchelli

CSS Publishing Company, Inc.
Lima, Ohio

WATCH THIS!
CYCLE C SERMONS FOR PENTECOST DAY THROUGH
PROPER 17 / ORDINARY TIME 22 / PENTECOST 12
BASED ON THE GOSPEL TEXTS

FIRST EDITION

Copyright © 2018

by CSS Publishing Co., Inc.

Library of Congress Cataloging-in-Publication Data
Names: Zuchelli, Dave, author.
Title: Watch this! : Cycle C sermons for Pentecost day through Proper 17,
    Ordinary time 22, Pentecost 12 based on the Gospel texts / Dave
Zuchelli. Description: FIRST EDITION. | Lima : CSS Publishing Company, Inc., 2018. | Includes bibliographical references and index.
Identifiers: LCCN 2018043903 (print) | LCCN 2018052820 (ebook) | ISBN
    9780788029332 (eBook) | ISBN 9780788029325 (pbk. : alk. paper)
Subjects: LCSH: Bible. Luke--Sermons. | Pentecost--Sermons. | Lectionary preaching. | Common lectionary (1992). Year C.
Classification: LCC BS2595.54 (ebook) | LCC BS2595.54 .Z83 2018 (print)
    | DDC 252 / .64--dc23

For more information about CSS Publishing Company resources, visit our website at www.csspub.com, email us at csr@csspub.com, or call (800) 241-4056.

e-book:
ISBN-13: 978-0-7880-2933-2
ISBN-10: 0-7880-2933-9

ISBN-13: 978-0-7880-2932-5
ISBN-10: 0-7880-2932-0

PRINTED IN USA

Contents

Show Us The Father

Philip put forth what seemed like a really good request. "Show us the Father." He added, "That will be enough for us" (John 14:8). Yes, that would be great. If we can just see the Father, we'll be cool. We'll have all the inspiration we need to keep plugging away. We'll be set for life. We'll be good.

This reminds me of the old Steve Martin movie, "The Jerk." There's a scene in which Navin (Steve Martin) is breaking up with his wife, Marie (Bernadette Peters). She tells him to leave, so he begins to walk out of the house. He announces to her that he doesn't need her or any of the stuff they've accumulated as they've grown wealthy together. But as he exits, he says, "I don't need anything...except this," and he picks up an ashtray.

As he makes the long shuffle out of the large room and down the hallway to the front door, he begins to pick things up along the way. Each time he picks something up, he says things like, "I don't need anything except this ashtray...and this paddleball." "I don't need anything except this ashtray, this paddleball, and this remote control." By the time he walks out the front door, he has an ashtray, a paddleball, a remote control, a box of matches, a lamp, and a chair. That's all he needs.

It's a classic, funny scene. It's one of those scenes that sticks with you over the years — long after you've forgotten the rest of the movie. It's also a scene that can remind us of our penchant for wanting more. We've got this, this, and this. If only we had one more thing, we'd be good.

Years ago, a very young cousin of mine made an astounding (and to us, a humorous) observation. The family had just installed a swimming pool in their backyard. In a very serious tone he announced, "Now if we just had a TV satellite dish, we'd be the perfect family." Yes, that was all they needed.

Jesus was preparing his disciples for his departure. He was only hours away from his passion and death. He had poured his life into them for the past three and a half years. He had announced to them he was going to the Father and would prepare a place for them. They weren't grasping what he was trying to tell them.

Thomas told him they couldn't follow because they didn't know where he was going. Jesus replied by giving him that famous answer from John 14:6-7. "I am the way and the truth and the life. No one comes to the Father except through me. If you really know me, you will know my Father as well. From now on, you do know him and have seen him."

It was at that moment Philip made his request to see the Father. Jesus must have been exasperated. He essentially shot back, "How can you ask that? If you've seen me, you've seen the Father!" His statements in reply to Philip help formed the cornerstone of our understanding of the Holy Trinity. He and the Father are one, and they would send the Spirit.

It was one of those moments of incredulity. After spending all that time with them, after teaching them everything they needed to know, and after he announcing his departure, they still had no clue! There were mere hours left in his life. There was little or no time to beat it into their heads. It must have felt like the first laceration of the scourge he was soon to experience (or the first spike through his wrist).

They needed one more thing. They needed to see the Father. They needed reassurance. They needed guidance. They needed...

As it turned out, they had everything they needed — at least for the time being. Jesus had imparted every bit of knowledge that would be necessary for them to make the next leg of their earthly journey. Their new pilgrimage had begun, and they were about to turn a corner. The rest of their trek would be without the physical presence of our Lord.

They thought they knew their need. They articulated it clearly, and I'm sure they were hoping Jesus would supply them with the answer they were seeking. Philip was, undoubtedly, speaking for the rest of them when he informed Jesus of their need to see the Father. In their confusion, they were grasping at straws.

We're not told if they understood him when he asked, "Don't you believe that I am in the Father, and that the Father is in me?" (John 14:10). He implored them to believe that it was true; if for no other reason than on the works he had done. He added that, if they believed, they would do even greater works than the ones he had done. I'm sure that sounded as unbelievable as anything he had said up to that point.

He told them so many things in these waning moments; it must have been impossible to comprehend any of them. But the most important thing he told them was this: "And I will ask the Father, and he will give you another advocate to help you and be with you forever — the Spirit of truth." I doubt they understood that at the time either. It was, in fact, the answer to their real need. They thought they needed to see the Father. What they needed, however, was to be indwelled by God's Holy Spirit — the Spirit of truth.

How could they remember all of these things? He seemed to be dumping heaps of knowledge on them without a chance to absorb what he was saying. They were mere men. How could they remember everything, let alone grasp it all? The task was beyond their abilities — particularly at a bewildering time such as this.

Jesus tried to reassure them by telling them he would not leave them as orphans — parentless in a hostile world. He told them he would come to them, and though the world would no longer see him, they would see him. These words made him more of an enigma than ever.

His final thoughts in this dialog provide us with his plan. His strategy included sending them an "Advocate." That Advocate was to be the Holy Spirit. They would remember things that otherwise would have been more easily forgotten. He said, "But the Advocate, the Holy Spirit, whom the Father will send in my name, will teach you all things and will remind you of everything I have said to you" (John 14:26). John could not have recorded all the words found in his gospel had the Advocate not been sent. It would have been humanly impossible.

On the day of Pentecost almost two thousand years ago, 120 disciples were gathered in a room. They were praying and waiting. They were cowering in their fear that the Roman army would find them. They were, after all, the followers of Jesus who the Romans had crucified only days before. That same Jesus, raised from the grave, had told them they would "receive power when the Holy Spirit" would come upon them (Acts 1:8). His word was true.

Pentecost is a high Jewish holy day. It is a season of the harvest, the day of firstfruits. Jewish pilgrims from all over the known world would travel to Jerusalem to celebrate God's blessings with one another. That particular year, however, Pentecost would take on a new meaning. It was the day the Father sent the Advocate — the Spirit of truth. It was the day the disciples had inadvertently asked for when they felt the need to see the Father.

When the Holy Spirit descended upon those in that upper room, everything changed. They finally discovered what it meant to see the Father. They began to realize what Jesus meant when he told them that he and the Father are one. They began to understand that they actually would do greater things than Jesus because the power of God had come upon them.

There were tongues of fire, sounds of rushing wind, and miracles of unknown languages being spoken and understood. They rushed out into the streets with a message infused with new life. Peter, who had denied Jesus only a few weeks prior, stood before the thronging crowds to preach a simple message of salvation through Christ. Empowered by the Spirit, his words rang true for three thousand souls who were added to the number of believers that day. With this newly imparted power, the fledgling church was off and running. In some miraculous way, the Holy Spirit had shown them the Father.

For many reasons, the Holy Spirit of God has become a controversial subject for many in the Christian world. There are myriads of questions surrounding the advent of personal Pentecost in the lives of many believers. Ask these questions of anyone, and they'll give you a different set of answers than the person before or after.

The one question that no Christian disputes, however, is this: Is the Holy Spirit important in the life of the church? The resounding answer is the Holy Spirit is not only important, but the Holy Spirit is indispensable. Without that descendant power, the church could not exist. Without that power, the church could not be a witness in this world. Without her witness, the church is nothing.

On the day Philip asked his infamous question, Jesus began to wrap up that part of the conversation with these words. "Peace I leave with you; my peace I give you. I do not give to you as the world gives. Do not let your hearts be troubled and do not be afraid" (John 14:27). He does not give as the world gives. He gives the Holy Spirit — the best gift of all.

Because the Holy Spirit now resides within the church (never to depart), we have that peace which passes all understanding. We can heed the words of Christ when he admonishes us not to be afraid. Our hearts don't have to be troubled because we have the assurance of salvation and the authority to live lives worthy of the high calling of Jesus Christ. Jesus ascended on high and gave good gifts to his children. We are those children, and we are his witnesses.

We have seen the Father. He is in Jesus and Jesus is in him. They have sent the Holy Spirit to reveal the triune God to our hearts. May we always walk in the grace, truth, and power of that same Spirit. May today be a fresh Pentecost for each of you.

Trinity Sunday/First Sunday after Pentecost
John 16:12-15

Three In One

One of the most difficult ideas in the Christian faith is the concept that God is three persons in one being. We call that triad the Trinity. The actual term, Trinity is not in scripture, but the idea is all over the place. It began in Genesis when the Spirit of God hovered over the waters (v. 3) and God said, "Let *us* make mankind in *our* image..." (v. 26) It stretched through to Revelation 22 where we see the "throne of God and of the Lamb" (v. 1) and the "Spirit and the bride say, 'Come'" (v. 17). The "Lamb," of course, is Jesus; and he shares the throne with his Father.

Many non-Christians (as well as a few Christians) have a difficult time with the idea of the Trinity. When the church first burst onto the scene, many people (particularly the Jews) in the surrounding cultures believed these Christ-followers to be polytheists, believing in three gods, not merely one. Today we have the "Jesus only" folks as well as those who believe that the Trinity is merely God manifesting himself in different ways.

At best, the Trinity is a difficult concept. We try to explain it through various means. We use metaphors such as the egg (yolk, white, and shell=one egg), the human being (I can be a father, a son, and a brother but still one human being), or water (ice, steam, and liquid — all H_2O). No explanation is perfect. No example covers it all. We just keep plugging away and do the best we can to explain the unexplainable. The Catholic Church has simply referred to it as the "mystery of the Trinity."

The church fathers did their best to describe what they were seeing in scripture. The concept of the Trinity is certainly there. The question was always, "How do we believe in one God and still hold all three entities together?" The Bible is clear in that there is a Father, a Son, and a Holy Spirit. Jesus, in fact, told us before he left that we should make disciples and baptize them in the name of the Father, Son, and Holy Spirit. So the church has done its level best over the years to recognize three Persons in one God — now known as the Godhead.

The apostle Paul probably did as much to help us grasp the fact that there are three persons in one God as anyone. Throughout his epistles to the church, he made references such as the one in Galatians 4:6 where he said, "God sent the Spirit of his Son into our hearts, the Spirit who calls out, *"Abba*, Father." His benediction in 2 Corinthians 13:14 stood out as another example of the Trinitarian understanding: "May the grace of the Lord Jesus Christ, and the love of God, and the fellowship of the Holy Spirit be with you all."

In our passage for today, John recorded the words of Jesus as he was preparing to die. He had one final meeting with the twelve. At one point in the conversation, Jesus seemed to wrap it up and said, "Come now; let us leave" (John 14:31). They didn't leave, however, and he went on to speak and pray for what we now identify as three more chapters.

I can remember times as a child when my parents would invite people over to the house. It was not unusual to hear someone say, "Well, we've got to get going." My Mom would go to one of the bedrooms and bring out all the coats. We would see everyone to the door, and the conversation would meander on for another half an hour. For a young kid, these were the visits that never seemed to end.

I'm not sure this was what was going on with Jesus and the disciples, but it definitely had that feel to it. Jesus wrapped up the conversation but realized there was much more to be said. He knew he needed to move on to what would be his final destiny in his earthly life, but he had more wisdom to impart to his followers. He also decided to stop and pray for them (and us).

In the midst of that, he admitted to the disciples that he still had a lot more to say — "more than you can now bear" (John 16:12). At that point, he reiterated to them that he would be sending the Holy Spirit — who he referred to as the Spirit of truth. That Spirit will "guide you into all the truth" (v. 13). This is a theme that runs throughout his discourse with them during the evening.

Jesus didn't stop with the Holy Spirit, however. He went on to say the Spirit would glorify him (Jesus) by receiving the words of Jesus and making them known to the disciples. By doing so, he established the relationship between himself and the Holy Spirit. Still, there was more to come.

He said something very telling in verse fifteen: "All that belongs to the Father is mine. That is why I said the Spirit will receive from me what he will make known to you." So the Holy Spirit receives from Jesus "all that belongs to the Father" because all that belongs to the Father belongs to Jesus as well. The Spirit, in turn, makes these things known to the apostles in order to glorify Jesus. What we end up with is a covenant relationship among the Father, the Son, and the Holy Spirit. They are a community within themselves, but they are one God. They are independent yet interdependent.

They are, obviously, three different persons; but they are not three different Gods. The early church had no other way to describe this relationship within one God as three distinct persons in one being (or of one substance). If you understand all that, you're doing better than most of us. The Catholic Church did the right thing when they called it the mystery of the Trinity.

One simplified way of looking at it is through the following generalization: Jesus was sent to earth to reveal God's love for humanity and glorify the Father. Jesus left and he and the Father sent the Holy Spirit to reveal and glorify Jesus. The Holy Spirit, as we have seen, was present in the Creation with God — hovering over the waters — much like a mother hen hovers (or broods) over her chicks.

As I pointed out, this is really an over generalization. Still, it's a handy way to remember how the three persons relate to one another (as well as to us). Trying to grasp the nature of God is no simple matter, but as we attempt to get a handle on things, we can certainly come to a better understanding.

In Creation, for example, we have seen the presence of the Holy Spirit. We have heard God (the Father) say, "Let *us* make human beings in *our* own image." Later in the prologue to his gospel (John 1:1-18), John indicated that all things were made through Christ. All three are present, all three are Creator, and all three are in existence prior to the "beginning."

Another piece of this amazing puzzle is the fact that we were created in God's image. That could mean a lot of things (and surely does). But one of the distinct possibilities here is that the Triune God created triune people. God is Father, Son, and Holy Spirit. Human beings, according to the apostle Paul, are body, soul, and spirit (1 Thessalonians 5:23).

We've only scratched the surface of this topic, but frankly, it took the church over three hundred years to officially establish and define the doctrine of the Trinity. Obviously, the idea and concept of it had been developed long before that, but it was hazy in the minds of most Christians. If it took that long for the church to formulate it, we're not going to do it justice in one short sermon.

It's helpful to note that there is no singular passage of scripture that is going to, flat-out, state the doctrine at which many of us have arrived. If there was, we wouldn't be having this discussion. You can't point to one verse and say, "See! That proves there's a Trinity." While many of us accept the doctrine, there are still many people (Christians included) who wrestle with the entire concept. It's not an easy one, to be sure.

For many, the question is not so much, "Is there a Holy Trinity?" The real question becomes, "What does that mean for us? How should this affect the way we live and respond to the living Lord?"

I think the first answer to that lays in the fact that God, within God's self, is in a covenant relationship. It is quite obvious that the relationship among the Father, Son, and Holy Spirit is an extremely close one. While they seem to have different functions, they rely heavily upon one another. They are interdependent in their actions as they support one another's roles. While the

Trinity is in covenant relationship with each other, the Lord is also in covenant relationship with us.

Beginning in the book of Genesis, we see God entering into covenants with his people. Because of that, we are even known as God's covenant people. The five major covenants of the Old Testament (Adamic, Noahic, Abrahamic, Mosaic, and Davidic), along with the New Testament covenant of love, form and shape us as God's people. As his covenant people, we share in the same love and mission as our covenant Lord.

The second effect the Trinity has on us as human beings is related to the first. The Trinity is not only in a covenant relationship, it forms a community within itself. The fellowship which exists among the Father, Son, and Holy Spirit is a picture of what the perfect community would look like. We might not ever be able to attain that kind of community in this life, but we have an example of what it can be.

There is a repeated call to community throughout scripture. We are called to be in community with God. We see this from the beginning. Adam and Eve existed in close communion with the Lord. But it doesn't end there. We are also called to be in community with each other.

When we read the early chapters of the book of Acts, we get a sense of what this can be like. The early Christians took their sense of community very seriously. They looked out for one another, worshiped together, and broke bread in each other's homes. They were a force to be reckoned with because they were a force for love. Their love was generated and fulfilled as a part of a Christian community that sought after the things of God. They followed Jesus, were inspired by the Holy Spirit, and glorified their Father in heaven.

The Trinity is our best model for all that can be good within us. The Trinity gives us our potential to be people of the covenant, and harvesters in God's vineyard. As we grasp what we can of the Trinitarian concept, let us live — body, soul, and spirit — as unto the Lord.

Proper 7 / Ordinary Time 12 / Pentecost 2
Luke 8:26-39

Selling Out

When I was in Israel several years ago, I took one of the boats that crossed the Sea of Galilee. When we reached the far shore, we were whisked by bus to a place near the ancient city of Gadara. In its heyday, Gadara was an urban area — one of the cities of the Decapolis. It was at the southern end of those Ten Roman Cities of fame.

Gadara is no longer a city. In fact, it is nothing but a few ruins now. The place of interest for us weary pilgrims was nothing but some rocky crags. Nearby stood the ruins of a cathedral that St. Helena had built hundreds of years ago. They were barely recognizable, but the edifice was constructed to mark the spot where Jesus cast demons into swine and sent them to their death in the sea.

The Golan Heights (the place of a strategic victory for Israel during the Six-Day War) can be viewed from this spot. While we were there, one of our guides (who had actually fought in that battle) told the story of the miracle that brought them victory. It almost overshadowed what had happened there two thousand years prior.

In the rocky crags I had mentioned, there were caves and tombs. They had been the dwelling place of the man we often call "The Gadarene Demoniac." He had lived among the dead — naked and demon possessed. The townspeople knew him well, and they steered clear. He was uncontrollable and violent at times. The Bible tells us that he and Jesus crossed paths as the Lord was passing through the area.

Jesus recognized the demoniac's condition and healed him of the demons. In a strange twist of the story, the demons begged Jesus to allow them to inhabit a nearby herd of pigs. Jesus acquiesced, and the pigs rushed into the lake and drowned. The pig herders ran off into town to tell the story.

Curiosity seekers made their way from the town out to the area of the tombs and found the man "dressed and in his right mind." (Luke 8:35) They were afraid (presumably because of the power Jesus had displayed) and asked Jesus to leave. Again, the Lord acquiesced. As he left, the man of the tombs wanted to go with him. Jesus denied his request, telling him he should go home and testify to the goodness of God.

This story has always seemed to draw a variety of reactions from Bible scholars. Some just think it's a strange story. Others have used words like bizarre and ludicrous to describe it. It's certainly not a sophisticated tale. It's more likely to summon the derision of skeptics than believers in the reality of scripture. I seem to remember a one-word commentary that came out, "Yuck!"

Since three of the four gospel writers include this story, there must have been a high value placed upon its telling. And, while demonic activity isn't the most pleasant of subjects, casting them out certainly offers a good view of the power of the Messiah.

Scripture flatly states that this man was demon-possessed. He wasn't merely oppressed or bothered by them. He was out-and-out possessed. That's strong language — even for the Bible. The townspeople were not able to bind the demoniac — not even with chains. His strength had to be as fierce as he was wild. In Mark's gospel, he is pictured as being extremely self-destructive — constantly shouting and wounding himself with stones. On top of that, Luke adds that he was naked. He must have been quite a sight. Today, we would look upon him as a prime candidate to be institutionalized in a prison for the criminally insane.

The demoniac lived in and around the caves and tombs I had seen in my pilgrimage to the Holy Lands. These were, undoubtedly, pagan burial sites. For a Jew, this would merely add to the uncleanliness of the entire situation. Any self-respecting Jew would avoid this guy like a plague. He was an unclean man living in an unclean place and filled with all kinds of unclean spirits. It doesn't get much messier than that. If you looked up the word "untouchable" in a Jewish dictionary, his picture would be right beside it.

It's interesting to note that, in many parts of the gospels, people don't seem to know who Jesus happens to be. They might have known his name. They might have known he was a carpenter from Nazareth. They probably recognized him as a Johnny-come-lately preacher type. But they never seemed to recognize him as Messiah. Jesus' family, his disciples, and certainly the Pharisees were in the dark as to who he really was. For the most part, they couldn't even take a good guess. And yet, here was this demoniac who recognized him right off the bat.

Shortly after bumping into him, he fell at Jesus' feet and screamed, "What do you want with me, Jesus, Son of the most high God?" (Luke 8:28) Then he begged Jesus not to hurt him. Can you imagine being an innocent bystander in that scene? I'm guessing it was a bit uncomfortable to say the least. No one else knew who Jesus was, but some alien spirit recognized him immediately.

Then Jesus did something probably no one else would do. He asked the name of the demon(s). Why bother? I've never heard a good explanation for this, but it helps us to understand the severity of the demoniac's problems. The answer was "Legion" because "many" spirits had entered him.

What happened next was even more curious. The evil spirits begged Jesus not to cast them into the "abyss." If we look at the same word for abyss in the book of Revelation, it connotes a place where demonic types are imprisoned. I guess that's an understandable request. The weird part, however, is that Jesus acquiesced and allowed them to enter into a herd of pigs grazing nearby.

The pigs immediately rushed down the hillside and threw themselves into the water. Apparently pigs are not good swimmers (at least not these ones), and they drowned. I'm not sure what happens to demons when their host's bodies pass from this life, but we never hear from them again (at least not in this story).

To understand a tad better what happened to the man in this story, we should take a quick look at the name given by the demons. Legion was a common term. In a country occupied by the Roman Empire, everyone knew what a legion was. A Roman legion could number up to as many as six thousand foot soldiers. They must have been quite a sight as they marched by, flanking each other.

Unfortunately for our friend in this short piece of history, I doubt if his legion of demons was marching in step. They were probably all over the place, going every which way, and tearing him apart inside. His had to be a miserable, agonizing existence with all that turmoil erupting inside him.

Even today, we hear stories of people who hear voices in their heads. Not only do the voices tell them what to do, they sometimes issue conflicting commands. Some people experience multiple personalities within themselves. Our demoniac must have been worse off than Mr. Jekyll and Doctor Hyde.

All this changed, of course, when the demons left him. He seemed back to his normal, pre-demon self. The townspeople heard the story from the pig herders who had witnessed everything. They made the trek out to the tombs and found their old friend calmly sitting at the feet of Jesus. He was now fully dressed and (as the Bible indicates) "in his right mind." Instead of conveying their happiness for the man and gratitude to Jesus as we might expect, they became fearful and entreated Jesus to leave their country.

There are probably a couple of good reasons for their fear as well as their request. First of all, Jesus just did what none of them could come close to doing. They couldn't control this guy, but Jesus not only controlled him, he cast out the demonic powers that were messing with their friend. Who has that kind of power? Anyone who does is certainly to be feared.

Secondly, those pigs had to have belonged to someone. They were somebody's property. Whoever the owner(s) happened to be (probably a consortium of townspeople), they lost a lot of capital. As we know, pigs don't fly. What's worse is they don't grow on trees, either. I'm sure they were concerned about Jesus' seeming penchant for drowning swine. If he hung around too long, they would be broke and destitute. If Jesus tried that today, he'd be sued.

I once heard a story about a group of Christians who were getting together each week to pray that the neighborhood bar would close down. Apparently, it was a nasty place that attracted lots of shady characters and was a festering pot for crime. They had approached the owners of the bar about it but had been laughed out of the joint.

One night the bar was destroyed when a monster storm came through and toppled a huge tree onto the roof. It wasn't insured, so the owners lost everything. Not knowing what else to do, the owners sued the group of Christians for praying against their bar. The Christians countering argument was simply, "Do you really think there's that much power in prayer?" Go figure...

There was obviously a lot of power in Jesus' prayer. The demons were gone, the man was in his right mind again, and the pigs were dead. If you sue Jesus, he has no defense. Short of suing him, you ask him to leave town.

Scott Peck was a psychiatrist who authored the books, *The Road Less Traveled*, *Further Along the Road Less Traveled*, and *People of the Lie*. In his practice, Peck began to come across people who he ultimately believed were demon possessed. Because of this, he studied these subjects intensely.

The upshot of his studies caused him to believe that demonic possession is rare. He believed that it was the culmination of a long, slow process. He concluded that it involved some cooperation on the part of the victims. This long process, he postulated, was one in which an individual sells out to evil repeatedly over time. If Peck was correct, Jesus' demoniac friend must have been selling out for years.

We have seen people who start by making simple compromises with one kind of evil or another. Initially they retain a measure of control. Bit by bit, their ability to stave off temptation erodes. After continuing to practice evil over a long period of time, they lose their ability to even care. Their conscience is seared, the chinks in their moral armor broaden, and they become open to the malicious forces that ultimately begin to take over.

Peck believed that these cases require more than normal therapy. His experience told him that the evil had to be confronted, and that it could not be dealt with or defeated until it was opposed. That's exactly what Jesus did in the passage concerning the Gadarene demoniac. Usually, Jesus is very understanding and compassionate toward sinners. In this case, he was extremely confrontational. That confrontation proved to be the key to his victory over the demonic power in the man's life.

In his gospel version of this story, Luke added that all the people of that area wanted Jesus to leave. He was gracious and conceded to their wishes. They were more comfortable with the status quo than with his presence.

That's where we come in. As we follow Christ, we watch and emulate him. We look around us in the world, and we see evil. It's more comfortable for us to go with the flow — to maintain the status quo. We're not interested in seeing Jesus hang around — or for us to hang around either. We're more interested in our comfort. Like the innocent bystanders in the clash between Jesus and the demons, we are made uneasy by the confrontation. We'd rather Jesus just not interfere.

The truth of the matter is this; we should be prepared to follow in the footsteps of the Savior. It's not often we see evil in the lives of others. Yet when we do, we could be confronting that evil before it takes hold of their lives. A gentle word here or a compassionate gesture there can make a world of difference. It's never pleasant, but it's a far cry from the heavy lift when things have gone too far. It's also the right thing to do.

The more evil grows in this world, the less popular the church will become. If we sell out to our own comfort, we will make it far worse for ourselves in the end. When our neighbors get comfortable with the status quo (the evil that surrounds them), they begin to hate those who stand against it.

In many Christian denominations and congregations, membership vows are taken. Among those vows is often one that states that we will stand against evil in whatever guises it presents itself. If we live up to that vow, we could be instrumental in staving off a growing evil in some person, situation, or (ultimately) in our culture.

When Jesus got off the boat that day, he was confronted by pure evil. Maybe it's time for us to step off our boats — our arks of safety. The folks wandering around the tombs just might need us.

The Steady March Forward

Some people get distracted by almost anything. As focused as I can often be, I'm also one of those guys who can walk from one room to another and forget why I went in there. I remember once, when I was about twelve years old, my Dad gave me some money to go pick up a loaf of bread. I hopped on my trusty bike with the basket on the handlebars and set out for the convenience store a mile or two down the road.

When I got there, I looked around to grab the... Uh oh! I couldn't remember what my Dad had sent me to buy. I walked up and down the aisles trying to jog my memory. I finally settled on a box of donuts. I have to say, my Dad wasn't the least bit happy with me.

Today's gospel passage (Luke 9:51) tells us "Jesus resolutely set out for Jerusalem" (NIV). The King James Version puts it this way — "he steadfastly set his face to go to Jerusalem." Fortunately for us, he didn't allow anything to deter him. Unlike me at twelve years old, he always knew where he was headed, and he always understood his destiny and destination.

That's not to say there were no distractions along the way. There were plenty of them. Remember where we are. Luke told us Jesus "set his face" in chapter nine. As Luke laid out his gospel narrative, he didn't get Jesus to Jerusalem until chapter nineteen. A lot happened in those chapters.

The road to Jerusalem was fraught with all kinds of occurrences. He was rejected by the Samaritans, turned down some would-be followers, visited Martha and Mary, drove out some demons, argued with some Pharisees, predicted his own death and resurrection, told a lot of parables, healed some lepers and at least one blind man, visited Zacchaeus, and finally rode into Jerusalem. The entire time he was doing those things he was continually teaching his followers the way of the kingdom.

With all that going on, it would have been easy for anyone to lose sight of their goal. Jesus, however, was not just anyone. He never lost sight of where he was headed, and he never forgot who he was.

As was his practice, he sent some of his followers ahead of him. They were what we, today, would call "advance men." They prepared the way for his arrival. They probably found some lodging and announced to people that Jesus was on his way. The message was a simple one — "The kingdom of God has come near to you" (Luke 10:9).

Jesus told them to shake the dust of the town off their feet if they were rejected. James and John must have been feeling their oats, for when they were rejected by the Samaritans, they wanted to call fire down upon the town and destroy it. Jesus would have none of it, of course, so they simply shook the dust off their feet and went to the next village.

The route they took to Jerusalem was not a direct one. They traveled from village to village and town to town. As they zigzagged across the countryside, not everyone rejected him. Some wanted him to stay. As he told them, however, there were other lost sheep that needed to hear his word. "I must proclaim the good news of the kingdom of God to the other towns also, because that is why I was sent," he told them (Luke 4:43).

People wanted him to stay for many reasons. He was a man of compassion, and he was a man of power. Put those two traits together and you get miracles of healing and tenderness. They weren't used to being treated like that by anyone with authority. The miracles, however, weren't his main purpose. After he had taught them, he moved on — on to the next village or to the next town. Jerusalem always loomed before him.

When he refused to remain in their towns, some followed him to his next destination. They wanted to be near his side, to hear his teaching, and to feel his compassion. They weren't sure who or what he was, but they knew he was someone special, and they wanted to be near the action that was sure to happen wherever he traveled.

He often attempted to discourage people from following. He seemed to do this when he saw their sense of adventure but their lack of commitment. He knew his road was a hard one with many discomforts. It would end with his death and their grave disappointment. He knew some wouldn't last when the wonderment wore off. They would return home to their comfort and safety. He, apparently, didn't want them to waste their time.

To them he said, "Foxes have dens and birds have nests, but the Son of Man has no place to lay his head" (Luke 9:58). He was basically asking them, "Is this how you want to live? Do you have that kind of commitment? Will you follow me through to the end?" He told all who would listen that if they looked back, they weren't "fit for service in the kingdom of God" (Luke 9:62). Most people would have jumped at the chance for a few extra followers. Jesus wasn't that way. He was looking for people who would stick with him through the end.

What juxtaposition! There are those whom Jesus called with a simple, "Come, follow me." There were no requirements, just a willingness to follow. Others begged to follow him, and he rejected their requests. The difference was that they had their own requirements and stipulations. If they were to have followed him, they wanted to do it in their own way and on their own time. What they didn't realize is it was God's kingdom, not theirs. They weren't in charge — Jesus was. They don't set the rules — God does.

Things haven't changed much in that regard. Jesus still calls us to follow him. Those who hear the call begin to die to themselves and look to Jerusalem. Others would like to follow without hearing that call. They don't last because they want to follow according to their own rubrics. That often means they'll follow him from a distance where things seem safe and comfortable. They want to be close enough to receive the glow but far enough away to avoid any problems.

As time went on, the true disciples must have been growing excited. They were headed to the Holy City (albeit through a rather circuitous route). Jesus seemed to be ramping up his teachings about the kingdom of God. What would happen when they reached Jerusalem? Would Jesus then set up an earthly kingdom while displacing the Romans? He certainly had done some amazing things up to this point. Why not that?

They seemed to ignore his statements that he was going to die. We like to call that little maneuver "denial." They heard what they wanted to hear, stayed close to Jesus, and wished for the best — at least, the best as they understood it. One wonders what their actions would have been had they actually believed Jesus was headed there to suffer and die.

On the night he was betrayed, Jesus surrendered to the authorities in the Garden of Gethsemane. Seeing the disciples' reaction to the events of that night, one might guess they would have abandoned him earlier had they known what was coming. A less likely scenario might be one where they kidnap Jesus themselves in order to keep him from going into the city. However wild that may sound, it's unlikely simply because he would still have gone eventually.

Given these possibilities, it makes me look at myself (as well as my contemporaries) in a much different light. It causes me to contemplate my own fitness for service in the kingdom of God. We all try to put our hand to the plow, and virtually every one of us looks back from time to time. I know I do.

The only thing that keeps many of us headed toward Jerusalem is the promised kingdom. Were it not for that promise, many (if not all) of us would turn and run. We'd deny Jesus, pack our bags, and head for the hills — or more probably, for our comfort zones. If we're really walking with Jesus, the discomfort of our journey can be truly discouraging. Looking back from the plow and furrows can be immeasurably tempting.

Everything was copacetic while the friendly and excited crowds were growing. It had to be exhilarating as they headed into Jerusalem on that first Palm Sunday. Adoring fans lined the road and proclaimed Jesus to be King. A few short days later, things had taken a drastic turn for the worse. How could this be?

These turns of events occur in our current lives also. Things are great when all is well, we're praising God together, and we're enjoying the celebration of life. These mountaintop experiences never last very long, however, and we're dumped into a valley of questioning and despair. Looking back can be very comforting while walking through the valley.

For Jesus' followers, walking throughout the countryside must have been a wonderful comfort zone. In the towns and villages, small crowds gathered, eager to hear the words of the Master. If they weren't so receptive to Jesus' compassion and message, they could simply shake the dust off their feet and move to the next burg. Not so with the city…

City folks are often a different breed. They are more skeptical. They tend to go with the latest fad. When one doesn't pan out the way they'd hoped, they move onto the next. In Jerusalem, Jesus became a quickly fading relic of an exciting day they had experienced earlier in the week. His lack of action proved him to be far less than they had imagined him to be (at least in their eyes). He wasn't pushing back on the Romans, and his words and actions gave no indication of a coming kingdom.

Worse than simply moving on, many of them grew hostile. To them, Jesus had not simply become passé, he was a threat to the peaceful order the day. The Jewish leaders were not excited by the Palm Sunday parade, and they did their best to rile up the masses against him. No, the city was definitely not the place to be. It was not the disciples' idea of a safe space. It was way out of their comfort zone. Yet, Jesus had now arrived at the place to where he had been headed all along. He could not be dissuaded from his appointed task. He was worthy and fit to serve in the God's kingdom. Yet, even he asked to have the ominous task before him removed. "May this cup be taken from me," he cried (Matthew 26:39). Despite his human agony, he resolved to do the will of his heavenly Father.

What confusion must have reigned in the hearts and minds of his followers — particularly the apostles? They must have felt like they were living in some surreal nightmare. They wanted to wake up and have it be gone. Unfortunately, they were all too awake. The discomfort of those moments must have called everything into question for them. It was too late to look back. They were caught in the now.

We all have these moments in our lives. We all have our doubts, our fears, and our misgivings. In our days of weakness, we are reminded of the call to set our faces toward Jerusalem — to remain resolute in the things of Christ. It's not easy being a disciple in the twenty-first century. It never has been easy. The early disciples were the first to discover this truth.

As we grow in our Christian faith, we understand more and more that there are things we need to do (as well as other things we should avoid). As our pilgrimage through this life winds through the villages and towns of our existence, we slowly gain confidence in the ability of Jesus to get us to the New Jerusalem. We ultimately learn that many legs of the journey will be hard, and there will be things we'd just rather avoid.

Yet, we tackle these hardships — these uncomfortable interludes — because we have learned we are part of something much larger than ourselves. We are part of the Body of Christ — the kingdom of God. The distractions along the way are merely that — distractions. They are not the sum total of our lives. They are merely obstacles to be hurdled, gone around, or obliterated. Despite them, it's on to the New Jerusalem.

My guess is we often have times of denial much like the early apostles did. We don't want to know God's will for our lives. Ignorance is bliss. We can't be responsible for what we don't know, right? There's a big problem with the life of a disciple. When we're following Jesus, it's quite clear that he often takes us to places we don't particularly want to go.

After the resurrection, Jesus had a stunning interlude with Peter. It was one during which many of us feel that Peter was forgiven and healed of his times of denial. During that conversation (found in John 21), Jesus told Peter that he would be led to a place he didn't want to go. He followed that up by saying to Peter, "Follow me" (John 21:19).

I doubt Peter wanted to hear that bit of news. Still, he grew in the things of God and learned to tread the path along which the Holy Spirit led him. He set his face toward the kingdom of God. He went to that place he quite possibly feared the most, and he conquered his fear with the aid of God. He was victorious in Christ.

This is the call that each of us has on our lives. As we set our faces toward the Holy City of God, we need to look for God's will and not deny it. We need to read and understand the Scripture — God's holy word. We need to surround ourselves with the Body of Christ

— the Christian community. We need to evaluate our thoughts, plans, and lives with his will in mind rather than giving in to our own, small whims.

As Jesus told us in his Sermon on the Mount, "But seek first his kingdom and his righteousness, and all these things will be given to you as well" (Matthew 6:33). It's not always the easiest thing to do. It most certainly comes with a degree of discomfort. Nevertheless, it's always the right thing to do. Set your face toward his kingdom. Can you hear his voice? "Follow me."

Lambs And Wolves

In last week's lectionary passage (Luke 9:51-56), we were told that Jesus set his face toward Jerusalem. This didn't mean he was making a beeline toward the city, but it was clear the Holy City was his goal. Many things happened along the way to the cross. He met hundreds of people, taught most of them, and healed many.

He did this by moving from village to village, and town to town. We don't talk about it much, but this isn't something he did in a helter-skelter manner. It appears that, after his disciples and followers had received a fair amount of preparation from him, he began to send them out ahead of him. From what we can tell in scripture, Jesus would send them out as advance men of sorts to the towns and villages to which he was about to travel. He sent them in pairs and gave them some pretty wild instructions.

First of all, he warned them that there was a large harvest out in the hinterlands, but there were very few people going into the harvest field. The obvious reference was to his view that there were a lot of lost souls out there that needed his compassion, his embrace, and his forgiveness. He apparently wanted to have the widest, most effective preaching tour possible. If a lot of people needed reaching, he wanted to make sure he had a fighting chance of personally touching their lives.

The second part of this warning was a prod toward prayer. He told them there weren't many people working on this harvest, and they should ask God to "send out workers into his harvest field." This may sound a bit strange to us since they, themselves, were the ones going out into that field. It almost sounds like they were to pray for their own success — maybe to have the courage to actually complete the task. Either that or they were to pray for helpers to aid them in their task. Either way, prayer was a prerequisite to the onset of their mission.

His next warning was a bit scary. He told them he was sending them out like "lambs among wolves." The metaphor was quite obvious. They were going to be at the mercy of the very people they were trying to serve. If you couple this warning with Jesus' admonishment for them to be "as shrewd as snakes and as innocent as doves" (Matthew 10:16), you get a pretty good picture of how they were to operate on this earth. They were not to go out in naiveté. They were to be worldly-wise yet vulnerable. They were to be totally open to the people they were going to serve yet be fully aware of the dangers they faced in doing so. This was no easy task. Their best example of this, of course, was Jesus. They had learned from the Master.

To ensure their vulnerability and dependence upon those they were to encounter on their journey, Jesus had a few other requirements for them. They were not to take any extra baggage — no "purse or bag or sandals" (Luke 10:4). This meant they didn't have a change of clothes, nor did they have any money to purchase anything.

That entire proposition sounds ridiculous to us. In their society, however, it wasn't out of the ordinary for people to travel and expect to find hospitality in the abodes of their countrymen. Houses were often constructed with an arrangement where the family stayed upstairs while the animals were housed below. Total strangers seeking refuge could be invited to sleep with the animals — and often were.

Jesus told them to stay with the ones who invited them in, and not to "move around from house to house." This would give them ample opportunity to invest their lives in a few people by getting to know them, earn their respect, work with and for them, eat with them, heal their sick, and learn to love them. Jesus understood the importance of investing in people's lives. Earning their love and trust was a precursor to gaining a positive avenue to share the good news.

I find it interesting that Jesus also added this instruction. When they were traveling to their destination, they were not to "greet anyone on the road." The only possible reason I can see for this directive would be for them to avoid any distractions — anything that could possibly sidetrack them from their appointed objective. Like Jesus who had "set his face toward Jerusalem" (Luke 9:51 KJV), they were to set their faces toward the town or village to which they were sent. They were to be purposeful and focused.

Their ultimate end, after they had won the love and respect of the people to whom they were sent, was to tell them "the kingdom of God has come near to you" (Luke 10:9). Their instructions appeared to be a lot of hoops to jump through just so they could relate that simple phrase. It's quite obvious Jesus placed a high value on earning the right to preach the gospel. It wasn't to be done willy-nilly or on the run. Passing along the good news of Jesus was to be an intimate transaction, not a drive-by shooting. Grabbing someone by the collar and announcing, "Jesus saves!" was not going to cut it. They had to win hearts before they could win souls.

Interestingly enough, Jesus did not guarantee them total success. In fact, he told them that when they were rejected, they should shake the dust off their feet and move on. Jesus, himself, was rejected more than once. He reminded them of that by saying, "Whoever rejects you rejects me..." (Luke 10:16). At least one group of Samaritans rejected him simply because he was heading to Jerusalem (Luke 9:53). People will reject us for many reasons. We shouldn't take it personally when, after having done our best to minister in the name of Christ, our efforts are rebuffed. If we've loved them and they still resist us, ultimately it's not us they are turning away — it's Jesus they're refusing to receive.

If we look closely, we'll also note that the approach was important. When they entered someone's home, they were to pronounce "peace to this house" (Luke 10:5). There was no prerequisite to this pronouncement — no precondition. It was to be freely given. Juxtapose this with James' and John's desire to call fire down on a Samaritan village that had rejected the Lord (Luke 9:54). Jesus rebuked them for copping that attitude. Shaking the dust off your feet is a far cry from heaping burning coals on the populace. Our mindsets toward people really seem to matter. If we're simply looking for another notch on our gospel gun, we're going about it all wrong. Everything Jesus told us points toward an attitude of love for those to whom we're sent. Anything less falls short of the goal.

Still, after all they had learned through this experience, their excitement was over the fact that "even the demons" (Luke 10:17) submitted to them in the name of Jesus. Though happy over their success and the fact that they had learned much, Jesus gave them a midcourse correction of sorts. He warned them that having spirits submit to them was not a particularly great cause for rejoicing. He told them the real cause for rejoicing was that their "names are written in heaven." Scripture doesn't tell us what their attitudes were in receiving that slight admonition, but I doubt it curbed their enthusiasm for what they had just experienced.

The disciples' experience as advance men for Jesus can be instructive for us all. Every one of us is an advance person for the Lord. It's our privilege to be such. He certainly doesn't need us, but it seems to be his good pleasure to involve us in his work of reaching people. We have opportunities in daily life to prepare the way for his arrival into the lives around us who need his touch. We, too, should be praying for workers in the harvest field — for workers like ourselves and for others as well.

People need to hear the basic message that the kingdom of God is near to them. They need to sense the love of Christ in us rather than any condemnation we might otherwise feel toward them. They need the sense that we are sent from God out of his love for them rather than as an object of some personal victory for us personally. If our name is written in heaven, it should be our desire that others should join us there.

Our attitude toward them means a lot. It's an attitude change that can only be brought about by a renewing of our minds (as the apostle Paul urged in Romans 12).

We need to be aware that, when we follow Jesus into the lives of others, there will be rejection — there will be costs involved. At times there will be no place to lay our heads, no time for goodbyes, and no time for funerals (Luke 9:57-62). Looking back will not be a viable option, but setting our face toward the high calling of Christ will be our posture.

We need to understand that investing our lives in those around us will be a priority. It will be exhilarating at times and deflating at other times. It will be a daily journey and a lifelong calling. It will be daunting and challenging, but our burden will be light. It will be so because we are yoked with Jesus who leads, guides, and strengthens us every step of the way. It will be so because we are empowered by none other than God's Holy Spirit.

We will discover that the forces of hell cannot stand before us. Those forces cannot defeat us, and they cannot deter us *if* we remember who it is that is in us. Satan will fall like lightning from heaven, and we will rejoice with our new brothers and sisters whose names are being written in heaven. We are like lambs among wolves, but we will win the day through Christ who strengthens us. Wolf-like fangs and claws are no match for the resurrection power of the one who resides within us.

Blessed be his name!

The Lawyer

"You jerk! What kind of question is that?" That might have been my response if I had been Jesus in that moment when asked, "And who is my neighbor?" The question was obviously a set-up. This expert in the law was trying to trip him up to catch him in some sort of "gotcha" moment.

This was typical of his exchanges with the legalistic types — the Scribes and the Pharisees who were hung up on the law without regard for the Spirit behind it. They were so protective of their territory; they weren't interested in hearing something that may threaten their status. They were the religious gurus, after all, and no one could stand before their guile, cunning, and knowledge of the law. No one, that is, until Jesus came along.

Jesus was really good at turning their questions back on them. He was asked what a person must do to inherit eternal life. The Bible tells us this was a "test." Jesus, undoubtedly, immediately recognized this as a trap. This expert in the law already knew the answer. What's more, he also knew he was probably in the company of some who believed in resurrection and others who didn't. Depending upon how Jesus answered, he was bound to make an enemy or two.

Jesus wisely turned the question back on this lawyer type. He phrased his question in terms of the law —

the questioner's area of expertise. He asked, "What is written in the law? How do you read it?" (Luke 10:26). Mr. Attorney couldn't back down from that one and quickly blurted out his learned answer. "Love the Lord your God with all your heart and with all your soul and with all your strength and with all your mind, and love your neighbor as yourself" (Luke 10:27). It was straight out of the textbook (the Bible).

Jesus commended him for his correct and straightforward answer. The legal expert wasn't about to let it rest at that, however. He quickly added his follow-up query about who his neighbor happened to be. This, in fact, may have been what he was getting to all along. The textbook wasn't quite as clear on that subject.

As he often did, Jesus responded by telling him a story. We know it as the "Parable of the Good Samaritan." As we all know, everyone loves a good story. The expert in question was probably a tad less thrilled than most, but he seems to have listened with interest. His intent was likely to find a flaw in the narrative Jesus was weaving. Not only did he fail to find a weakness in the story, but Jesus also compelled him to answer a final follow-up question of his own.

I sometimes wonder if Jesus crafted these parables on the spur of the moment, or if he had a store of them at the ready. I suppose it may have been a bit of both, but they were certainly effective. The Good Samaritan has not only stood the test of time, but most people (including many who've never read any scripture at all) know who the Good Samaritan happened to be. Some probably know the story but don't realize where it came from. I wonder how many have attributed it to Uncle Remus.

Regardless of how (or when) he came up with it, the Parable of the Good Samaritan was a piece of genius — a thing of beauty. Like most of his other parables, its brilliance lies in its simplicity and straightforwardness. Anyone can understand it — even those whose minds are closed. Our lawyer friend was certainly cut to the quick by its unavoidable truth and sincerity. The cast of characters was contemporary and real, and the action was well within the realm of plausibility. In short, our resident expert in the law had nowhere to run.

The parable begins with a guy traveling down from Jerusalem to Jericho. It was an authentic bi-way that everyone knew existed. Undoubtedly, many of them had traveled it. I, myself, have ridden from Jerusalem to Jericho on a bus. Let me tell you, it's no picnic. I had the privilege of getting to ride on a paved highway, of course, but it's through rough, dry, hot, sandy, rocky terrain. I wouldn't want to have traversed it on foot the way most folks did it in Jesus' day.

The road Jesus was referring to was not the same one as my highway. Google it, sometime... It's still there. The pictures of it are worth a thousand words (make that a million). It's narrow, up and down, along rocky ridges, and often treacherous. It was nicknamed, "the Way of Blood." As Jesus told his story, it could not have been a surprise to his listeners that the traveler was beset with thieves and thugs who beat him up. It earned its nickname the hard way.

Many places all along that road were conducive for the bad guys to hide and ambush any passersby. Their only surprise may have been that the man in the story seemed to be traveling alone. Not a good idea. A winding, meandering trail like that one would be dangerous even if there were no highwaymen lurking around.

So, the man is left naked, bleeding, and dying along the side of the road to Jericho. He could have lain there a long time before anyone came along. However, Jesus places three other men on the road that day. The first to happen by, according to Jesus, was a priest. One might surmise the priest was headed toward Jerusalem to take his turn at the priestly Temple duties. If that was indeed the circumstance, the case could be made on his behalf that he needed to maintain ritual cleanness. Messing with what could be a dead body would defile that cleanness, and his trip would be made null and void of its intended purpose. I'm sure Jesus would not have accepted such an excuse, but there it is. Scripture tells us he steered clear of the dying man by heading on down the opposite side of the road.

Enter man number two. The second guy is identified as a Levite. The Jewish priests were part of the tribe of Levi, but not all Levites were priests. The remainders were, however, a part of the holy proceedings of temple worship. Some of them took part as singers in the temple choir. Others were musicians who played instruments as part of the worship music. Many of the Levites whose talents were not in the field of music were designated to be temple guards. In any case, this particular Levite may well have been headed to Jerusalem to participate in holy worship as well. He, too, would have found it necessary to remain in a state of cleanliness. Thus, he passed the dying man by moving to the opposite side of the road.

In the cases of both the priest and the Levite, they were either assuming the man was dead, or they weren't going to take the chance he could die while they were helping him. Even if he was alive, they were leaving him for dead. The law was on their side, after all, and they had a perfect excuse to remain uninvolved.

One other possibility exists that may explain each of their failures to check more closely on the wounded traveler. That possibility was simply that the whole thing could have been a trap. The beaten man could have been used as a lure to entrap other passersby. The thieves may well have been lurking behind some nearby rocks, and the priest and Levite were merely being cautious — erring on the side of safety. Who can blame them for that? After all, they were traveling alone as well.

Whatever their reasons, these two upstanding Jewish men did nothing to help their "neighbor." Whether they assumed it was a lost cause, a catastrophe waiting to happen, or a mission not worthy of the trouble it may entail, they didn't stop. Their insensitivity to the plight of their fellow traveler set the stage for the third man to arrive on the scene.

That third man, of course, was the person now known famously as the "Good Samaritan." The adjective, "good," is not in the original story. Most Jewish countrymen would not have put the words, "good" and "Samaritan," in the same sentence (particularly to use good as a modifier to Samaritan). The Jews and the Samaritans summarily hated one another. The reasons for this ran deep and stemmed from events dating way back in history. Suffice it to say, the Jews were accustomed to referring to their Samaritan neighbors as dogs and half-breeds. The Samaritans didn't show a lot of love in return either. If anyone in this story was likely to pass by the half-dead victim, it was the Samaritan (at least, Jesus' listeners would have assumed as much).

Lo and behold, the Samaritan stopped to see if the man was alive, he covered his wounds (probably using his own clothing as bandages), poured his own oil and wine onto the bleeding areas (thus sanitizing, cleansing, and treating the wounds), and transported the man on his own donkey to the nearest inn. On top of that, he gave the innkeeper two denarii. One denarius was about a day's wages at that time. He asked the innkeeper to take care of the man, ostensibly nursing him back to reasonable health. He added that he would be back on his return journey to cover any extra costs that may have been incurred in the process. Such sacrifice is generally known to many of us as "going above and beyond the call of duty."

Scripture indicates the Samaritan had "pity" on the man. I'll say... He placed himself in danger, gave up two day's wages, used his own resources, and went out of his way to see that the man was well cared for. He apparently wasn't too worried about any ritual cleanness, either. What a guy!

After unloading this story with the wild twist, Jesus then looked to his trusty lawyer friend once more and asked, "Which of these three do you think was a neighbor to the man who fell into the hands of robbers?" (Luke 10:36). Well, what would *you* say? What *could* he say? His answer was the only logical one left to him. There's one final note to this encounter, however.

I'm pretty sure I would have simply answered, "The Samaritan." The legalist, being a true lawyer, had a slightly different, slightly longer answer. He said, "The one who had mercy on him" (Luke 10:37). I might be reading a little more into this than is present in scripture, but it seems like he couldn't bring himself to use the word, Samaritan. It could be that his prejudice and hatred ran so deeply, it would be difficult for him to even utter the name in such a positive light. To his chagrin (and possibly to his shame) he identified more closely to the priest and Levite than he did to the Samaritan. He knew (deep down inside) that he would have passed by on the far side of the road.

Jesus put the final nail in the lawyer's un-neighborly coffin by telling him, "Go and do likewise" (Luke 10:37). There were no arguments left to wield. Jesus had left him without a leg upon which to stand. He knew he'd been had.

Now it comes down to us. There's no sense in us asking Jesus who our neighbor happens to be. Our neighbor is anyone and everyone in need of our help. We don't have to be Samaritans or lawyers to see that. Jesus' words ring down through time to our listening ears, "Go and do likewise."

I Need

My lovely bride and I used to laugh about our youngest daughter's use of the phrase, "I need..." It seems as though she never simply wanted things — she "needed" things. At one point in her life, these two words became her mantra. "I need this dress. I need a car. I need to go out tonight. I need..."

I don't mean to pick on her, because I'm sure most other parents go through a similar stage with each of their teenagers. They all *need* something. Interestingly enough, their actual needs are already being met (in most cases). It's their wants that are sometimes in question. Then they extrapolate those wants into needs.

Truth be told, however, most of us are pretty good at doing that — adults included. I occasionally find myself needing something. Frankly, I already have everything I need. But, if I want it badly enough, it seems to become a need to me. (Please, don't tell my daughter I admitted that.)

In today's passage, we find a situation full of needs. Jesus is out on the road. He and his disciples are traveling from village to village, teaching and preaching. It was customary for the traveling teacher to find shelter with one of the villagers. Since Jesus was traveling with his disciples, they had a pretty good-sized group to be entertained. I'm guessing hospitality had its limits —

even in those days and in that culture. So, I would suppose they were quite grateful when they found a willing host — or, as it was in this case, a willing hostess.

The hostess was a woman named Martha. At this point in the story, we don't know a lot about her. She apparently had a good and generous heart. Feeding Jesus and his band of merry men couldn't be all that easy (not to mention, costly). She did it, however, and there doesn't seem to be any whining about having shouldered this burden.

The one thing we *do* know is that Martha had a sister. Whether or not they lived in the same home, we're not told. It seems pretty apparent, however, that they lived in the same village. They probably had many things in common, but, like many siblings, they had varying priorities.

Since Jesus had come to the village to teach and preach, he didn't waste any time. As he settled into his new situation, he began to expound upon whatever the topic of the day happened to be. It's likely that a small crowd quickly gathered and Jesus, no doubt, got on a roll.

Martha and Mary were both intent on hearing what Jesus had to say as, undoubtedly, all the other folks within earshot were as well. A *need*, unfortunately, arose within Martha. According to scripture, she became distracted. This is not an uncommon occurrence. We all have our distractions, but Martha's distraction ends up making her look like the bad guy (or gal) in this gospel story.

Martha realized that, if all these people were going to get fed, something had to be done. There were preparations to be made. Vegetables had to be cleaned.

Meat had to be cooked. For all we know, an animal had to be slaughtered and dressed. These are, after all, important distractions. Yea for Martha! It's a dirty job, but someone's got to do it.

One supposes she could have waited. Everyone else seemed to be satisfied with cooling his or her heels, listening to the Master. 'Everyone else' included her sister, Mary. What's a girl to do?

At first blush, our reaction is to side with Martha. We've all been there. I can remember times when I've invited guests to my home for dinner at six. Everyone gets there at five and lounges around in the living room, yakking it up. The closer it gets to six, the more distracted I become. I duck out several times to check on the roast (or whatever), make sure the salad is mixed, and freshen up the drinks and hors d'oeuvres. There have even been times when I've said, "Hold that thought until I get back."

I'm guessing Martha didn't feel comfortable saying that to Jesus. Most people don't ask me to pause my sermon while they take a potty break or check on their child in the nursery. So, there she is. She either makes the preparations, or dinner will be late. She decides to be the good hostess and make the preparations.

Somewhere along the way, Martha realizes she's missing out on some good stuff. This is Jesus, after all. How often does the Messiah pop in for dinner? You don't want him to starve, but should you have to sacrifice the main reason why he's here? You want that spiritual food as much as the folks reclining in your living room do. Why should you miss out?

With this going through her mind, she begins to fume. She realizes her sister, Mary, is soaking it all in while she, Martha, is slaving away in the kitchen. It really gets to her. She *needs* Mary to help. It's just not fair. Why should she be the one to miss out? So, she decides to do something about it.

She marches out to the living room (or whatever room they used for such things in those days) and tells Jesus in no uncertain terms what he should do. And what he should do is, "Tell her to help me!" (Luke 10:40). I should think it would take a little pluck and audacity to give Jesus that directive. She was really angry with her sister.

But Mary was not the only one with whom she was furious. She prefaces her instruction to Jesus with, "Lord, don't you care that my sister has left me to do the work by myself?" She was obviously a little ticked off at him as well. It reminds me of the time when Adam (in the Garden of Eden) blamed Eve while pointing a finger at God by telling him it was that "woman *you* put here with me!"

I've tried putting myself in Martha's place, and I'd like to think I would have caught myself at that point. I'm not really sure I would have, but I'd certainly like to think so. It would have saved a considerable amount of embarrassment on her part. She didn't catch herself, however, and the embarrassment ensued.

Before we go any further, let's take a momentary look at Mary. She doesn't get named much in this story (twice), but she definitely plays a major role. All she does is sit at the feet of Jesus. What do you suppose is going through her mind through all of this?

Here's what I think. Mary, being Martha's sibling, had a really good idea about what was going on in Martha's head. She had grown up with her, she knew her habits, she knew her foibles, and she knew how to yank her chain (so to speak). I'm sure Mary had a strong feeling that Martha was beginning to fret as she sat at Jesus' feet, struggling to listen to all he had to say. Still, Mary had a *need* of her own. She needed to relax and soak up everything Jesus was laying down. She probably knew how much it was eating away at her sister, but she didn't really care (they were siblings).

Here we have two women with their perceived needs. Jesus is caught in the veritable middle. Realizing the situation, he does something extremely out of character for him. He takes a side. One could speculate he did so because he became irritated with Martha's attitude. I seriously doubt that, though. I think he genuinely felt Mary was doing the correct thing.

In fact, part of his answer to Martha is that Mary was doing the one thing that was "needed." There's that word again. I'm sure Jesus did it tactfully and lovingly. Yet, he told her in no uncertain terms that Mary was right.

He reminded Martha that she was "worried and upset about many things" (Luke 10:41). That statement caused me to wonder as to whether he had taught on this subject while she was out of the room. He certainly had done it other times. In his Sermon on the Mount, he is recorded as saying, "Can any of you, by worrying, add a single hour to your life?" (Matthew 6:27). I guess it pays to stay in the vicinity when Jesus is speaking.

More importantly, he went on to tell her that only one thing is "needed." He never actually said what that one thing happened to be, but we all get his drift. He announced that, "Mary has chosen what is better. (Luke 10:42). What she (Mary) had received could not be taken from her.

I have to admit at that point, I would have become somewhat annoyed with Jesus if I had been Martha. Not only was he taking sides with my sister (who from my point of view had done zilch), he was also implying that what I was doing could be taken away from me — it could be lost. *Really?* I was the one waiting on him hand and foot and it amounted to nothing? In today's world I would have been thinking, "Shots fired!" I wouldn't want to get into it with the creator of the world, but it would have been quite tempting to do so.

Unfortunately for Martha, Jesus was exactly right. Her need to see that her guests were fed on time was, primarily, a desire. It may have been a desire driven by the traditions of her culture and society. Nevertheless, it was a mere *want* rather than a *need*. Her real need was to receive nurturing from the Savior of her soul. Martha, it seems, was a victim of her times. As such, she missed out on the Lord's best in order to provide him with something that would be gone in a short time.

This story is a microcosm of our lives today. Most of us are so busy fulfilling our desires; we seldom seek the satisfaction of our real need — the need for Christ. It's a theme we play and replay daily in our world. We chase after that which we want, escalating it into a need in our own minds. By doing so, we placate our consciences with the thought that we are only doing what the Lord would want us to do. Jesus loves us, therefore, we deserve it (or so we think).

We start with the correct premise. Jesus does love us. Then we veer off into areas he's not leading us. He loves us and wants the best for us. The best for us happens to be Jesus, himself. Our own desires, wants, and wishes seldom measure up to our real need (in fact, they never do unless those desires, wants, and wishes are for him).

But doesn't scripture tell us, "He will give you the desires of your heart"? Yes, indeed, it does. We like to quote that thought from Psalm 37:4. We'd rather leave off the first part of the sentence, however. The entire thing says, "Take delight in the Lord, and he will give you the desires of your heart."

If the Lord is our delight, he will also be our desire, our aspiration, and our stated need. In the context of Psalm 37, this verse makes perfect sense. The preceding verse also tells us to "trust in the Lord and do good." The following verse says, "Commit your way to the Lord." In essence, it relays to us the following proposition. If our recognized need is for God, many benefits will flow our way as a result.

We, of course, want these blessings to be handed out like candy at Halloween time. Just walk up to the door, say, "trick or treat," and the Lord will turn into Santa Claus (please pardon the mixed holidays). He will then meet all our perceived needs — just because. While we don't (and can't) earn our salvation, many of the blessings that follow come with a cost. Placing God first reaps many benefits. Merely pronouncing we need something doesn't seem to cut it.

We don't know if Mary had any desire to cook or assist Martha in any way. Secretly, she may have been sick of hanging around the kitchen taking orders from her sister. Maybe she was downright lazy. Or maybe, just maybe, she recognized the real need in her life. Maybe she saw an opportunity of a lifetime unfolding before her. Maybe she wanted that real need to be satisfied before she was willing to succumb to her desire to fulfill her customary role.

We make many decisions in life. Many choices lay before us each day. Some of those choices are ones in which we must choose between our wants and our needs. We begin treading on dangerous ground when we redefine the things we want into the things we need. Just remember... "Few things are needed — or indeed only one" (Luke 10:42). The best course seems to be considerably narrowed down. Choose Jesus. No one can take him away from you.

Shameless!

One of the reasons I want to preach on this passage of scripture is because I've never really understood it. The only way to really make sense of it is to view the story of the friend at midnight as a parable.

You may remember the old definition of the word, parable. It goes something like this. A parable is an earthly story with a heavenly meaning. We could flesh that out considerably, but this little quip really captures it quite nicely. Parables are sometimes confusing until you realize that most, or at least many, of them have one clear point — all the details not withstanding.

The stage is set for this parable when Jesus is apparently praying in a place where his disciples can hear him. His prayers seem somehow different than the prayers they know. The Jewish prayers of Jesus' day were primarily memorized and recited from rote. To this day, many Jewish people will avoid praying extemporaneously. The reason they give is that the standard, formal prayers cover the necessities. They also are a way of avoiding any mistakes such as forgetting someone or something as they pray.

Jesus didn't seem to do this. His prayers sounded much more personal. They sounded more heartfelt and passionate. His prayers were obviously something rather foreign to the ears of the disciples.

After hearing him pray (probably on more than one occasion), they certainly must have discussed the nature and source of his petitions. They weren't sure how he was arriving at this new pattern of going before God. Why was he doing it this way? More importantly, "Do you think he could teach us to do it like that?"

They asked him. "Lord, teach us to pray." They had precedent for doing this, because they somehow knew that John the Baptist had taught his disciples to pray as well. John, too, must have veered from the traditional way of lifting his supplications to God. They cited this knowledge by adding, "…just as John taught his disciples" (Luke 11:1).

Jesus, of course, acquiesced by teaching them a form of prayer we now commonly call "The Lord's Prayer." A lot has been said about the prayer he gave them (particularly the version recorded in Matthew 5:9-13). In fact, entire books have been written to explain its nuances and meanings. My sense is that it's less a prayer than it is an outline for prayer. If Jesus was praying in an extemporaneous way, as it seems he was, he would be reticent to give them another memorized formula for reaching out to God Almighty. They already had those.

If my theory is correct (and it's not entirely my own), Jesus was giving them bullet points on prayer. He was essentially saying to them, "Think about these topics as you approach the Lord in prayer and pray through them from your heart." It's ironic that we have taken those bullet points, memorized them, and turned them into a rote prayer. We all do it, and it's a rather lazy way to pray.

And that leads me to the friend at midnight. The story (or parable) is a brief one. Jesus puts his listeners in the position of someone needing food for his guests. They've arrived very late in the evening and quite unexpectedly. The surprised and (unprepared) host knocks on his neighbor's door. His neighbor is less than receptive. He's already in bed (as are his children), and he's not interested in getting up at midnight to help someone who could have easily been more organized for guests. Since the guy is still in bed, we can imagine the yelling that must have taken place:

Neighbor: ...*knock, knock*...
Friend: "Who is it?
Neighbor: "It's your next-door neighbor, Moshe!"
Friend: "What do you want?"
Neighbor: "Some company just arrived at my house. Can you spare me three loaves of bread? I'm fresh out!"
Friend: "Are you nuts? It's midnight! I'm in bed, and so are the kids. I'm not getting up just to give you my bread!"
Neighbor: "Please! I'd do it for *you!*"
Friend: "No way, Jose! I can't get up. I've got a long trip ahead of me in the morning."
Neighbor: "But, you're already awake. Just do this one little favor for me!"
Friend: "I can't give you anything!"
Neighbor: "Yes, you can. Please! Get up and help me out!"
Friend: "Okay, okay! I'm getting up. Stop your yelling, you disrespectful pig!"

Now, we've got to remember that Jesus was right in the middle of a discussion concerning prayer here.

He had just passed along the Lord's Prayer to his disciples. As a follow up, he told this bizarre story about a neighbor trying to scarf bread at midnight from a sleeping friend (at least he calls him "friend"). He ended the story by telling the disciples that the guy didn't get bread because he was a friend. He got bread because he's shamelessly audacious. Go figure.

Various English translations of scripture use words like persistence, impudence, shamelessness, importunity, and rudeness to describe why the neighbor ended up getting the bread. Literally (from the Greek), verse eight says, "Because of the prospect of being put to shame, he will get up and give him as much as he needs." At first blush, it almost sounds like Jesus is saying that we can shame God into giving us whatever it is we want. While it sounds like that, we need to blush again.

Let's go back to our original discussion of parables. Most of them make one point. The point of this one is not that we should try to shame the Lord into doing our bidding. It's that we know he has what we need, and we should go to him boldly to seek his favor. He further clarified this by his next couple statements.

In Luke 11:9, he postulated one of his most oft-quoted sayings: "Ask and it will be given to you; seek and you will find; knock and the door will be opened to you." Then, in verse ten, he added, "For everyone who asks receives; the one who seeks finds; and to the one who knocks, the door will be opened." And there it is.

He wants us to ask. He wants us to seek. He wants us to knock on the door. He wants us to be bold enough to actually believe that God will answer — that God will meet our needs (even at midnight). God is the one we should ask — the one we should seek — the one upon whose door we should be knocking. Far too often, we look for a different source.

Our sources are common. Sometimes, we think we can take care of every situation on our own. We can figure everything out. We can put on our thinking caps and arrive at the best solution. Other times, we try the wisdom of the world. Occasionally, we'll meet with the townspeople. Surely, they'll have an answer for us.

I think it bears being said that these various avenues may well be how God answers our prayers from time to time. But the point of the parable is this. We should go to him first. Because we are bold and audacious enough to believe he is the overall answer to any situation in our lives, he will answer.

How many times have we failed to receive an answer simply because we didn't ask? When we seek the Lord and persistently knock on the door of his heart, he will answer. He never tires of answering. He expects us to seek him, and he is more than willing to open the door (not just because he's our friend, but because we were shameless enough to go to him once again). If the neighbor doesn't ask at midnight, he probably doesn't get the bread.

We cannot stop there, however. Jesus is not finished with his dissertation on prayer. The disciples haven't heard everything he wants to say to them. There is one final piece of information he has to impart on that subject. And even though a lot of folks pass this part off as a little, extra add-on, it's the most important bit of info he could give them as they approach their prayer life.

In verses eleven and twelve, he asked them a couple of questions. "Which of you fathers, if your son asks for a fish, will give him a snake instead? Or if he asks for an egg, will give him a scorpion?" These are, obviously, rhetorical questions. Everyone knows the answer, and that answer is, "None of us!" He asked these questions to make a point. He asked these questions as a run-up to the final (and most important) instruction on how to pray.

Remember the initial quest. The disciples had come to him and said, "Lord, teach us to pray." The point he wanted to leave them with is contained in verse thirteen. He taught it to them (as he often did) in the form of another question. He said to them (and I believe to us), "If you then, though you are evil, know how to give good gifts to your children, how much more will your Father in heaven give the Holy Spirit to those who ask him!"

When you pray, address the Lord as your heavenly Father. Ask him to supply your daily needs. Seek his forgiveness and the strength to forgive others. Ask for the courage to resist temptation. But above all, ask him for his Holy Spirit.

This was his bottom line. This was his exclamation point. You know how to give good gifts to your children. Guess what! So does your Father in heaven. Ask him for a good gift. Be audacious enough to ask him for his best gift. Ask him to give you the gift of his Holy Spirit.

When you approach your good and holy heavenly Father, ask him to fill you with himself. Be persistent. Ask him daily. Not a day goes by that we lack the need for God's power in our lives. We never have enough strength, wisdom, and clarity to do everything on our own.

The disciples didn't realize what they were getting into when they said, "Teach us to pray." They thought they were going to receive a new technique — a different and exciting formula for success with God. What they finally received could be boiled down to one simple instruction. Ask your Father in heaven to give you his Holy Spirit.

We have, by and large, forgotten that instruction these days. It's gotten lost in the formulaic prayer we like to offer up as congregations each Sunday. It has been pushed aside as we seek to have the Lord bless the things we're already doing.

The call is clear. The instruction is simple. But the results are unknown. And that may be the very reason we've pushed this instruction aside. It's quite safe to ask for our daily bread. It's comforting to address the Lord as Daddy. It's a bit scary to ask him to fill us with his Spirit. After all, what might happen when the awesome resurrection power of God resides within us?

The answer is a resounding, "We don't know." Are we bold enough to ask? Are we audacious enough to seek? Are we shameless enough to want his best for our very own? I hope so.

How Did I Get That Job?

Apparently, Jesus wasn't crazy about the idea of helping people squabble over their possessions. Truth be told, Jesus didn't seem to be all that crazy about having many possessions in the first place. I once heard someone say that Jesus spoke more about money and possessions than about any other single subject (except for hell). Frankly, I don't know if that's true or not. I've never counted.

I suppose it's like a lot of things. It depends upon how you count things and what words and phrases you interpret as being related to the subject. Regardless, Jesus did have several pertinent things to relate to us on the topic. He was willing to teach them as general principles, but he wasn't interested in judging between two arguing parties — particularly when the argument was due to their own selfishness.

While he refused to be their arbiter, he didn't hesitate to fill them in on a couple tenets of the kingdom of God. He quickly warned them that greed could be their downfall. "Guard against all kinds of greed," he implored them (Luke 12:15). He gave a similar warning to the Scribes and Pharisees. In Matthew 23:25 he said to them, "Woe to you, teachers of the law and Pharisees, you hypocrites! You clean the outside of the cup and dish, but inside they are full of greed and self-indulgence."

The Matthew passage is part of a larger pericope in which Jesus pronounced seven woes on the teachers of the law and the Pharisees. A significant portion of those woes dealt with possessions, wealth, and/or physical treasures. When people got hung up over material things, alarm bells seemed to go off in Jesus' mind.

His reference to the cup and dish was directed at laws of ritual cleansing. The hypocritical religious types were eager to make sure the outside was spotless. Jesus, however, drew a distinction between the clean surface and the filth that lay within. That filth, in Jesus' mind, was their "greed and self-indulgence." They were careful to give an outward appearance of holiness while harboring avarice and hedonism inside. Jesus saw this as one of their major downfalls.

He, obviously, didn't want that kind of attitude to manifest itself in the two who were disputing the family inheritance. It mattered less to Jesus to whom the inheritance belonged than that their hearts were free of greed. The inheritance would be fleeting. Their greed, on the other hand, could destroy them.

Jesus pointedly tells them that, "Life does not consist in an abundance of possessions" (Luke 12:15). It's a statement that is reminiscent of the scripture passage that says, "Man shall not live by bread alone, but on every word that comes from the mouth of God." This passage is found in Deuteronomy 8:3 and is quoted by Jesus in Matthew 4:4 and Luke 4:4. It seems at every turn, Jesus downplayed the importance of material things when juxtaposed to the things of the heart and of God's kingdom.

As is usually the situation, Jesus didn't leave it as a simple admonition. He added a parable to drive the point home. In this case, it's the story we have come to know as the Parable of the Rich Fool. Our fool in question is evidently a farmer. Not only is he a man of the soil, he is apparently quite good at it. He has had at least one or two good years (crop-wise).

Because of that, he decided the prudent thing to do is tear down his barns (which were ostensibly inadequate to handle his newfound success). In their place, he decided to erect larger ones. His new stash included enough surplus grain for a long time, so his attitude became, "Take life easy; eat, drink, and be merry." Where have we heard that before? (Actually, I think this is where that saying started.)

Most of us Americans would appreciate this guy's attitude. Work hard, save up, and sit back to enjoy the fruit of your labors. It seems, however, that Jesus is not your typical American. (Truth be told, the last time I looked, he wasn't American at all.) Does Jesus have it wrong? The rich man's end is not what we're hoping for at all.

God calls our thrifty, prudent friend a "fool." No fooling! How can that be? He did everything right. As far as we can tell, he invested in hard, honest labor. His time was well spent. He reaped far beyond his capacity to enjoy it all in one year. He wisely built structures to hold the excess, and he organized for the future. My financial planning friends would have been proud. God was not proud, however.

Why was this guy a fool in God's eyes? The simple answer was, "This very night your life will be demanded from you" (Luke 12:20). And there you have it. We are not promised tomorrow. All our plans for easy retirements and vacations in the sun can be laid waste in an instant. If we die, who gets it all? Not us, that's for sure. You may remember the old saying that announces, "There are no pockets in a shroud." Then there's the ever popular, "There are no U-Hauls hitched to the hearse." In the end, we can't take it with us. What a bummer!

It was certainly a bummer for our rich fool. He didn't even get one day's enjoyment from his grain haul. Where's the justice in that?

In recent years, we've put a little twist on Jesus' saying. The turn of the phrase is now, "Eat, drink, and be merry for tomorrow we die." That's a tad closer to the truth, but our rich friend didn't even get today. It was still today when he died. When tomorrow came, he was already lying in a tomb.

Most of us don't take kindly to this story. Frankly, we don't think it's fair. The guy deserved to enjoy some of his returns, didn't he? I'd like to think so, at least. But then, Jesus puts a capper on his parable that helps us get a handle on his main point.

It's not that it's wrong to save. It's not that it's wrong to be prudent with our wealth. It's not even that it's wrong to enjoy life. Take a look at how the Lord wraps things up in this story. He says, "This is how it will be with whoever stores up things for themselves but is not rich toward God." And there's the crux of the matter.

We should remember that parables are generally told to drive home one particular tenet. The idea behind this one had nothing to do with the man's shrewdness. It had everything to do with how he used his wealth.

His own pocket was his only target. Storing things up for his own benefit was his primary concern. Jesus obviously took issue with that focus.

He indicates that the man should have been "rich toward God." Instead of worrying about filling his barns, he should have been concerned for the things (and the people) for which the Lord is concerned. Jesus once said, "Where your treasure is, there your heart will be also" (Matthew 6:21). It's pretty apparent where this guy's heart was.

But where does that leave us? How do we become rich toward God? What does that even mean?

I think it means we need to develop a heart for the things of the Lord. If our concern is only for ourselves, we will fall short in life. If our concern is for others, we'll not only bless them, but we'll end up being blessed ourselves. If I have a thousand extra dollars and use it to feed the hungry, am I a thousand dollars poorer or have I just invested in the kingdom of God? Our personal answer to questions like that one will say a lot about where we stand with our wealth and possessions.

I once saw a bumper sticker that said, "He who dies with the most toys, wins." I'm pretty sure Jesus didn't have that one on the back of his donkey. It's anathema to everything for which Jesus stood. While it's no crime to be rich, Jesus had some rather stringent things to say about it. You've undoubtedly heard Jesus' saying, "It is much harder for a rich person to enter the kingdom of God than for a camel to go through the eye of a needle" (Mark 10:25). That statement is found in all three of the synoptic gospels, so it must be somewhat important for us to understand.

He also said, "But woe to you who are rich, for you have already received your comfort" (Luke 6:24). I really don't like the sounds of that. It more than implies we already have our reward and shouldn't expect anything further (like a home in heaven). So does that mean we have to give it all away and live like paupers?

I might be treading on dangerous ground here, but I don't think so. I think he's speaking as much about attitude as anything. We can work hard and amass a fortune. We may have even inherited everything we have. The problem is not that we have attained it. The real question is what are we going to do with it? How are we going to manage what we have?

I believe the reason it's so hard for rich people to enter the kingdom of heaven is because of the attitudes that so often accompany our riches. We get possessive. We begin to hoard what we have collected. We become overprotective of the things we have amassed. It's our stuff, and no one better try to separate us from it.

That attitude is a killer — literally. In Luke 12:48, Jesus said, "Much is required from the person to whom much is given; much more is required from the person to whom much more is given" (Good News Translation). The attitude of rich people can be one that says, "This is my stuff!" By way of contrast, the attitude of "Kingdom People" is one that realizes everything they have comes from God. In fact, everything we have is on loan from God. We are merely trustees.

God tells us in Psalm 50:10 that "every animal of the forest is mine, and the cattle on a thousand hills." We can either recognize that fact, or we can become misers, cheapskates, and hoarders; mistakenly thinking that it's all ours to do whatever we please. The main difference between a rich person and a poor one is responsibility. Every person is compelled by the Spirit of God to be a good steward of whatever they have received. Since the rich folks have received much more in terms of physical riches, they have a greater opportunity to be givers from that area of life. It appears that attitude is everything.

The real problem with our rich fool was his attitude. In his eyes, everything was his. He worked for it, he earned it, and he was going to do whatever he wanted to do with it. There was no thought of investing it in the work of the kingdom of God. There was no thought for anyone around him. There was no questioning as to what God's will may have been for his good fortune and extra blessing.

He did not see himself as a steward of what God had given. He saw himself as sole owner and proprietor — the head honcho — the big kahuna. He was going to do whatever he pleased, and that was that. Too bad for him his life was over. He didn't even have the blessing of a cheerful giver to carry with him to the grave. All he had was... Well, all he had was nothing. He had nothing to show for all his hard work and his miserly attitude.

We're all rich fools if we think we deserve everything we possess. In fact, we're fools if we think we actually possess anything. We're stewards of God's good gifts. We're trustees of his blessings to us. Someday, we will return all our stuff to him. We can either invest it wisely in the work of his kingdom, or we can make a valiant (but vain) attempt to hoard it all for ourselves.

Should we do the latter, we will end up becoming big losers (just as our friend the rich fool wound up becoming). There is no substitute for being rich toward God. It's a way of life, not a notion for the moment. It's an attitude, not a fleeting idea.

The storehouse is not ours. It belongs to God Almighty. If we attempt to live life merely in the abundance of our possessions, we will live shallow, sad lives indeed. If we live with dollar signs in our eyes, we will become the biggest fools of all. If fighting over an inheritance is our main concern, we're headed down the wrong pike.

Giving Away The Kingdom

One thing I learned a long time ago is that the Bible makes sense. Some things, of course, are mystical and difficult to understand. Other things seem fantastic and beyond the reach of reasonable explanation. But in the grand scheme of all that we find in scripture, everything begins to make sense as we see God's plan laid out before us.

With that in mind, when I hear Jesus say, "Sell your possessions and give to the poor," I have to wonder: Does he mean for us to sell everything? It seems like quite a blanket statement on the surface of it. "Sell your possessions" has no qualifiers. He didn't say, "Sell half your possessions," or "sell a tenth of your possessions." He merely said, "Sell your possessions." Frankly, it sounds like he wants us to sell it all.

It really doesn't make a lot of sense to do that. For one thing, if every Christian sold all their possessions and gave all the money to the poor, we would die out inside two weeks. I'm just guessing, but I'm pretty sure that's not the Lord's intent here. Being a guy who believes the Lord meant what he said; I've got to struggle with this one.

The apostle Paul once wrote to the Christians at Thessalonica and reminded them of a rule they had instituted while he was with them. It was a simple one.

"The one who is unwilling to work shall not eat" (2 Thessalonians 3:10). He also said something similar to the Ephesian church. He told them to do something useful with their hands "that they may have something to share with those in need" (Ephesians 4:28). These instructions seem to dovetail with what Jesus is saying in today's text.

Selling possessions and giving to the poor cannot be done unless we're earning a livelihood. If we're not working and producing, selling and giving things away will put us into the category of the down and out before too long. If we're all poor, we'll all starve. I'm quite sure that's not God's plan for the human race.

It sounds like Jesus and Paul want us to be productive and then be generous with what we've earned. In so doing, we will be investing in God's kingdom. Our treasure will be in heaven, and our hearts will follow. It sounds easy, but it takes a lot of courage to live like that.

Jesus understood this, which is why he led into our passage by saying, "Do not be afraid, little flock, for your Father has been pleased to give you the kingdom." In order to live a life of generosity, we must first place our trust in the Lord. We must have enough confidence in him that we expect him to come through for us. If our giving is significant, there will be times when we will be the ones in need. Do we trust God enough to provide in those times?

I've heard people say that we should live by faith in such a way that, if the Lord doesn't provide, we won't make it. That, my friends, is a life lived close to the edge. I'm not sure I would be very relaxed living like that. Like most of you, I feel more comfortable when there are a few dollars in the bank. On the other hand, when I'm invested in the things of God, my heart resides with him and my faith grows as I see him provide.

The passage leading into our scripture lesson for today is all about worry — more specifically, not worrying. Jesus is telling his followers that God will take care of their needs. It follows that, if we're trusting God for our own needs, we're not going to fret over helping someone else. We'll be able to do that without fear. We have a tendency to hedge our bets when we consider offering our hard earned dollars to others in need. Jesus is basically telling us to go for it — be generous. God's got our back.

While everyone was trying to absorb what Jesus was telling them, he launched into two short parables. At first blush, these parables seemingly have no relation to what he had just said about possessions. However, a closer look provides us with a deeper connection than first perceived.

The first story Jesus told concerns servants waiting for their master to return home from a wedding reception. They didn't know when he would get back, so they were admonished to be ready and on the alert for his return. Jesus noted that the man could arrive home at any hour of the day or night — even as late as daybreak. Still, the servants should be "dressed and ready for service" (Luke 12:35).

This story ties back into his previous parable about the rich fool (Luke 12:13-21) whose life was required of him before he got to enjoy the fruit of his labors. Like him, these servants are up against a timetable without a clock. They don't know when their services will be required. They just have to be ready when the time comes. The final line of the second parable explains the real meaning. "You also must be ready, because the Son of Man will come at an hour when you do not expect him" (Luke 12:40).

The tie-in becomes obvious when we think about our lives and our possessions in terms of time. We don't know when our lives will be required of us. We don't know when Jesus will return for us. Neither do we know how long we will have our possessions and wealth. Anything can happen. We've seen these things occur in the lives of others, and we could be next.

The question for us then becomes one of service. Are we in service to the master now, or are we waiting for some other time to be faithful with what we have? Are we currently using our means (our wealth and possessions) to be of service in God's kingdom? Are we investing in heaven now by coming to the aid of humanity? If we do the latter, we position our hearts with the Son of Man rather than with our own selfish desires.

The second of the two parables is virtually identical in meaning. It's only one verse long — one sentence. In Luke 12:39 Jesus simply states, "But understand this: If the owner of the house had known at what hour the thief was coming, he would not have let his house be broken into." The watchword of these two related parables is readiness. Be ready to serve at any time. Don't wait for some future date to be generous with your time, your wealth, or your possessions. That date might never arrive.

This, I suppose, begs a couple of questions: "When should we serve," and "How often should we be expected to give?" Verse 35 says everything we need to know about this. Be ready. Be prepared. Have the mind and heart of a servant twenty-four/seven. The idea is not to keep tabs on the number of times we give or the amount we offer. The idea is to be ready, willing, and able. If this is our state of preparedness when opportunities for service and giving arise, we'll be of a mind and heart to jump in to do our part.

The actual context for most of Jesus' teachings in Luke chapter twelve is a question posed in verse thirteen. Someone had asked Jesus to intervene in a dispute over a family inheritance. Jesus' immediate retort indicated in no uncertain terms that he was not an arbiter in such matters (nor did he care to be such). He warns the quarrelers against greed and tells them the Parable of the Rich Fool who dies. His overall point in all of what follows is this. If we're following Christ, our possessions are his, we are his, and our heart is his. What we own will become secondary. Everything we are and have will be positioned for service to our Lord.

There's a slightly different way of looking at this as well. That way is the way of expectation. When you're expecting someone, your heart and thoughts are with them. If we're expecting Jesus, we'll have a heart for his work. Our thoughts will be aligned with his will for our lives. Our possessions (including our very lives) will be implements of his grace, mercy, and compassion. We will be doing what we can to usher his kingdom into the lives of those around us. If he has won our hearts, the blessings he has bestowed upon us will be expendable in our quest to serve him well.

In verse 39, Jesus speaks of a thief. The owner of the house must be ready for the thief who would come and steal into his home. The Son of Man (Jesus) is not a thief of that sort. Yet, he steals our hearts. We want him to be near to us. We expect him to come. Thus, we are always ready and waiting for him to show up. We don't have to think about it, we just are.

And show up he does. He comes on our scene in so many ways. When we look into the face of a starving child, we see Jesus. When we put our arms around a woman whose heart has been broken by divorce, we are holding Jesus. When we help a wounded veteran put his life back together, we are helping Jesus. If we're willing to see Jesus in the faces, hearts, and lives of those around us, he shows up in myriads of ways. It's our calling — it's his voice echoing out across the circumstances of life.

Jesus is the love of our lives. As such, we recognize him as the real owner of the things we like to call "our possessions." They're not ours — they're his. We are merely trustees. He has entrusted us with blessings to be used in his work. The return is guaranteed.

When I was a credit manager for a large produce firm, I was introduced to the PACA statute. PACA stands for Perishable Agricultural Commodities Act. It was instituted by Congress to protect those who sold agricultural goods that had a short shelf life. The industry credit standard was *net thirty* (meaning the customers had thirty days from delivery to pay). The obvious problem is that the produce would be long gone by the due date — even if it went unused, it spoiled by then. That left nothing for the seller to reclaim or repossess.

The PACA law essentially put the produce into a trust. At the end of the thirty days, even though the original potatoes or bananas were gone, the trust remained. As a credit manager attempting to collect debts, this was a handy law. We seldom lost a case because of the automatic trust that was created by the initial transaction.

The Lord has given us possessions, which we similarly hold in trust. The restaurateurs who used our products in their menu items would earn enough money to pay us at the end of the month. They no longer had the produce, but they had the profit of their sales from which to pay their initial bill. Likewise, we can't pay the Lord back by returning his original blessings. We can, however, use those blessings to produce fruit for the kingdom of God.

When Jesus is the true love of our lives, we're always ready to serve him. We're waiting for the opportunities to do so. When he arrives on the scene, we're there to greet him — to tell him we love him — to offer our service in whatever ways we've been equipped to do so.

When Jesus is the love of our lives, our hearts belong to him. Our trust is in him and his provision for us. We are inheriting a kingdom — the kingdom of God. If we're looking to a bottom line, we can be assured that our assets will always outgain our losses. Jesus' opening words in the passage then become truly significant. "Do not be afraid, little flock, for your Father has been pleased to give you the kingdom" (Luke 12:32).

I've Come To Bring Fire

"I have come to bring fire on the earth, and how I wish it were already kindled!" (Luke 12:49). This is a pretty startling statement from Jesus. This is something we'd expect old Beelzebub to spew forth as he foamed at the mouth. It's not the kind of thing you'd expect Jesus to say. It is, undoubtedly, one of his least quoted utterances.

Out of context, it sounds as though he's about to bring hell on earth. When most of us think of a place called hell, we envision flames, torment, and punishment. These are not things we readily associate with the prince of peace — the wonderful counselor — the Lamb of God. As always, however, we need to place these words into context.

We discover at the beginning of the chapter, "a crowd of many thousands had gathered" (Luke 12:1). The same verse of scripture tells us there were so many gathered, "they were trampling on one another." Despite the size of the crowd, Jesus speaks first to his disciples. He warned them of the hypocrisy of the Pharisees. There were, undoubtedly, Pharisees gathered among those crowding in to hear him. A confrontation with them was almost inevitable when they and Jesus shared a space in close proximity to one another. Sure enough, Jesus would tee off on them before the day was over.

Someone attempted to get the Lord involved in a family dispute over an inheritance. Jesus would have none of it and admonished them to be on guard against greed of any kind. He fleshed that out by telling them the (now famous) Parable of the Rich Fool who built large barns to house his crops for retirement — then died. This grim tale set the tone for the afternoon.

As he taught the crowd that day, Jesus told them they didn't need to worry — God had their back. He told them to invest in God's kingdom rather than in treasures here on this earth. Stressing over material things wouldn't add to their lives in any way, he said. He added other parables that chided them to be wary and ready for service at all times.

Then he came out with the fire and brimstone statement. It may have been a shocker for many who were gathered there that day. He not only said he was going to bring flames to bear, but he wished out loud that the fire had already been ignited. He implied that the only reason this hadn't happened as yet was because of the "baptism" he was about to undergo. His hands were tied until he had gone through that baptism.

We can only speculate as to what the baptism was. From our side of the resurrection, it appears he must have been referring to his passion and death. He touched on it very fleetingly and didn't explain what he meant by it. He quickly moved on to say he had not come to be a reconciler but a divider.

This sounds way out of place for Jesus. He is called the great reconciler in other portions of Scripture. For example, the apostle Paul told us that God "reconciled us to himself through Christ" (2 Corinthians 5:18). In

Ephesians 2:11-16, he explained that Jesus had reconciled both Jews and Gentiles to the Father. Furthermore, he added in his letter to the Colossians 1:20 that the Christ had reconciled "all things" to himself. Why would Jesus call himself a divider?

He not only did that, he additionally explained that there would be disputes within families over him. "From now on there will be five in one family divided against each other, three against two and two against three. They will be divided, father against son and son against father, mother against daughter and daughter against mother, mother-in-law against daughter-in-law and daughter-in-law against mother-in-law" (Luke 12:52-53). This doesn't sound like the reconciling Savior we have come to know and love. What could he possibly mean by these things?

When in doubt, the best answer in these situations is simple. We have to assume he meant what he said. As hard a pill as it is for us to swallow, his language was plain and simple. His presence among us would drive a wedge between some people, and some of those people would be from the same family. He made no bones about it.

We live in times when division has become the watchword. We are split by culture. We are separated by status. We are delineated by class warfare. Candidates isolate us into voting blocs. Wealth (and lack of it) keeps us apart. Some of our own representatives in government have even called themselves "the resistance." In this kind of atmosphere, it shouldn't be all that difficult to understand what Jesus was driving at with these declarations.

We need to be careful that we don't try to turn Jesus into a one-dimensional being. He is a multi-faceted person even as we are. You and I can have friends and still make enemies. Each of us can be loved and hated at the same time by different people. While the bottom line for Jesus is always love and reconciliation, not everyone will follow him. Not everyone will believe on his Name. There will be some that will even dislike us merely because we are Christians. In those cases, the Lord himself is the source of division.

It's at this point in his teaching where he levels a barrage at the religious elite of his day. He mentions to them that they are good at discerning the weather. If they see clouds forming to the west, they predict rain (and they're correct). If there's a wind blowing in from the south, they predict a hot spell. Again, they're correct. We would think this would be a good thing, but Jesus turns it around on them.

He calls them hypocrites — phonies, frauds, charlatans. He asks them how they can predict the weather by reading the signs, but "How is it that you don't know how to interpret this present time?" (Luke 12:56). That sounds more than harsh to us.

How were they to know what Jesus was ushering in? Did he expect them to be clairvoyant? They were to know the same way they knew the coming weather. They had signs to read. Remember, these were the religious leaders of the day. They're the ones who studied, knew, and interpreted the scripture. All the signs were right in front of them. Jesus, himself, should have been the final sign, but they ignored him. They regarded him as a blasphemer and a false prophet.

Instead of opening their hearts to the Lord, they were hell-bent on opposing him at every turn. He was a threat to their status — to their prominence. They couldn't have someone like him showing them up. The promised Messiah hadn't shown up for centuries. Why should they think he had arrived on the scene in the person of Jesus? Why? — because, all the signs pointed to him. They were too blinded by their own privilege to see him for who he was and is.

That trend has never changed. That attitude still blinds people to this day. There are still many who look upon Jesus as the enemy — as someone who wants to take away the things they hold dear. They will oppose their own family members to take a stand against the ways of Christ and his teaching. They will look to any sign that can placate their own desires while ignoring the one who is *the* sign.

There is something we may want to take away from all this. When Jesus confronted the opposition in the crowd that day, he (in essence) took a stand that we don't have to take today. He took it for us.

By that, I mean it is not our job to call our enemies hypocrites. In fact, our job is just the opposite. Remember the Sermon on the Mount? In that most famous of all sermons, Jesus said, "Love your enemies" (Matthew 5:44 and Luke 6:27). We are called upon to be reconcilers, not judges.

When the apostle Paul talked about Jesus as being a reconciler, he added one important thing. He said, "All this is from God, who reconciled us to himself through Christ and gave us the ministry of reconciliation" (2 Corinthians 5:18). Did you catch that? He gave us the "ministry of reconciliation."

I don't know about you, but I don't have the time (or, frankly, the discernment) to go around calling out

God's enemies and judging them. Jesus has already pointed out their foibles. That's one of the reasons why they don't like him. My job is to love them. It's not easy, but it's my calling. I need to let the judging up to Jesus.

From where I sit, it looks like it's the job of every Christian to love others. Everyone who has answered the call of Christ has been commissioned to love. There is no limit or parameter to that love. We are to love everyone.

I have no doubt that Jesus loved the very people he called hypocrites as well. That could be why he was so harsh with them. He may have wanted to shake them out of their darkness and into his light. In John 9:5 he told us, "While I am in the world, I am the light of the world." He is no longer in this world. He left and sent his Holy Spirit. In so doing, he placed a mantle upon our shoulders.

He told us in Matthew 5:14, "You are the light of the world." That is certainly a heavy burden. Yet he was clear. He told us he would shoulder that burden alongside of us. His actual word to us was, "Take my yoke upon you and learn from me, for I am gentle and humble in heart, and you will find rest for your souls. For my yoke is easy and my burden is light." He's not asking us to do anything he isn't preparing us to do. Nor is he asking us to do any job at which he won't be doing most of the heavy lifting.

There will be times when we will see the task before us as impossible. The reason for that is simple. It *is* impossible. But with Jesus yoked to us, carrying the heavier part of the burden, the unmanageable becomes manageable. With him by our side, the onerous is softened. With him in our hearts, the arduous becomes a joyful experience.

He may well "bring fire upon the earth." But for us, it will be a cleansing fire. Come, Lord Jesus...come.

Disabled

It is no longer politically correct to use the word "crippled." We are now supposed to say "disabled." I get it, but the Bible was not written in (or to) twenty-first-century people. So please forgive me as I proceed to "kick against the goads" for a while.

Our scripture lesson for today begins with a woman "who had been crippled by a spirit for eighteen years." This passage poses a double dose of non-PC speech, since it's no longer cool to believe in demons either. Those nasty spirits have been reduced to quirks in people's personalities. You've heard many people say things like, "He's dealing with his demons." They don't really mean demons, they just like to misuse the word and give it a new understanding.

So in the new PCV (Politically Correct Version), Jesus is presented with a woman who has been disabled by some psychological disorder, addiction, or pervasive habit. Her demon of disability had her hunched over for eighteen years, and it seems no one could help her get straightened out (no pun intended).

Jesus was teaching in one of the local synagogues at the time and couldn't help but notice the woman and her prominent malady. Unlike other times in Jewish history, women were a prominent part of synagogue worship during the time of Christ. There was no separation of the sexes, and the women were counted among the number for the religious quorum (which happened to be ten). For this ailing woman to be present while Jesus was teaching was not an earthshattering event.

It did become earthshattering, however, when Jesus called her out of the congregation. I'm sure there was more than a little murmuring as the startled woman edged her way toward him. Things probably got really quiet when he said to her, "Woman, you are set free from your infirmity." There were undoubtedly all kinds of thoughts running through people's minds at that point. "Who does he think he is?" may have been foremost among those thoughts.

As if on cue, Jesus placed his hands on the woman. Scripture indicates that she "immediately" stood up straight. It's not clear in which town this occurred, but it was probably in one of the small towns and villages in Judea. In that case, everyone gathered for worship that day would have known the woman. They would have understood that her disability was real because they had seen her ambling along, stooped over for the past eighteen years. There was no question about the authenticity of the healing.

There was a lot of indignation, however. This incident took place on a Saturday (the Jewish sabbath). No work was allowed on the sabbath, and any self-respecting Jew would observe that law. The leader of the synagogue obviously felt that healing was some form of work. There were doctors of sorts back then. They were "physicians" who, at best, were people who used herbs, spices, and oils to attempt healing. At worst, they were shamans of a sort and used incantations and magic spells. Either way, they had to "work" to attempt a healing. So in the synagogue leader's defense, this judgment would have been correct in most other circumstances.

Jesus, of course, was no ordinary physician. In fact, he was not a physician at all. I know we like to refer to him as "the Great Physician," but he was in a class all his own (for obvious reasons). As it was, it could be argued that he was not doing any work in healing the woman (at least, not in the same sense as an ordinary physician would do). I often wonder why preaching and expounding on the scriptures was not considered work, but laying hands on a disabled woman was. Maybe that's why the rabbis sat down when they preached and taught. I suppose they looked more relaxed in that position.

Interestingly enough, the synagogue ruler wasn't audacious enough to attack Jesus straightforwardly. He made his remarks directly to the congregation. "There are six days for work. So come and be healed on those days, not on the sabbath" (Luke 13:14). So in essence, he generally laid the entire congregation low — and in particular, the woman with the eighteen-year demon.

I have a sneaking suspicion that the leader of this synagogue was a bit skeptical to begin with. He was probably looking for some slip-up on Jesus' part so he could jump in and save the day. He was the leader there, and he didn't want some stranger horning in on his territory. I may be way off the mark on that one, but it stands to reason. Jesus met with these kinds of attitudes almost everywhere he went. Why should this man be any different than most of the Scribes and Pharisees with whom Jesus butted heads wherever he taught. As we will see in Jesus' answer, the synagogue ruler was not the only one opposed to what he had just done.

Another aspect of this man's action may be a desire to stave off any further problem. If Jesus was, indeed, doing work on the sabbath, the ruler sure wouldn't want any more people getting healed. It would make no sense to permit this itinerant preacher to double down on his sin. The ruler couldn't just stand by in silence and allow others to step up to be cured. There were, undoubtedly, other disorders represented in the crowd. Wouldn't each of them want their demons removed? Nipping it in the bud may have seemed like the proper action to take in the heat of the moment.

Jesus, of course, would have none of it. He immediately spoke out — harshly, I might add. He uses the word, "hypocrites." Note the plural form here. Jesus is not merely speaking to the synagogue ruler. He is speaking to anyone who is in opposition to the healing of this woman. Apparently, there were several. He knows from experience it probably has less to do with the day of the week and more to do with trying to trap the teacher into making a mistake. What they were looking for was a big "gotcha" moment. He wasn't about to give them one.

Jesus pointed out that each of them didn't think a thing about untying his own donkey or ox and leading it to water on the sabbath. Isn't that work? Yet, they were more bent out of shape than this "daughter of Abraham" before she was freed from her bondage on that same sabbath. Hypocrites indeed...

Unlike other passages where we see Jesus casting out demons, very little is made of it here. He does, however, end this discourse by reminding his opponents that it was Satan who had bound the woman for the past eighteen years. Now, Satan has been evicted, the demon is gone, the woman stands upright, and the hypocrites are humiliated. Not bad for a day's work.

Political correctness aside, evil spirits can cripple any of us. There are spirits of greed, spirits of lust, and spirits of envy (just to name a few). In today's story, we see a spirit of legalism at work. The enemies of Christ were too bound by the law to stand by and let God work on the sabbath. As Jesus reminded a different group of people at another time, "The sabbath was made for man, not man for the sabbath" (Mark 2:27). To place the day above the dire needs of a human being is not God's way. Legalistically interpreting God's laws is a spiritual problem with which we all need to deal. It seems as though most of the religious leaders of Jesus' day were not willing to do so.

On the other hand, Jesus was anything but legalistic. His compassion (and maybe all human compassion as well) transcends the law. His detractors may have been technically correct. Still in the end, they were humiliated for their attitude. We can take a lesson from their stubborn adherence to the law even as it flies in the face of human decency.

The synagogue ruler's attitude is disturbing on most levels. He saw truth as being on his side, and he allowed it to make him insensitive to the disabled woman's plight. Healing may indeed be work, but the greater principle displayed by Jesus is his compassion. Thus, he is completely accurate (and within his rights) to use the descriptive word, hypocrites.

By his actions and words in this passage, Jesus is telling us that restrictions, laws, rules, and institutions can be important — even good. But if we aren't careful, they can keep us from the charity to which we are called. Compassion is always appropriate. Love God and love your neighbor. When you've accomplished those two things, you can point to your scribal laws — but not before.

Society has a way of dehumanizing us. We can become slowly desensitized to the plight of others around us. Increasingly, we fail to see the worth of humanity before a righteous God. The woman in Luke's story had been dehumanized. She had been reduced to little or no value to others. The laws of Moses had become more important in people's eyes than a disfigured woman. As much as the woman's back was bent, a legalistic spirit bent someone's soul even more.

Nothing can choke the heart and soul of our walk with God like legalism. I will be the first to admit that Christians should be disciplined. However, we can become so rigid in our beliefs that our disciplines can cripple us.

Does this mean we should chuck any and all of our rules? Of course not... Most of them are in place for a good reason. As long as that reason is still in existence, the rule is probably effective and necessary. But we should never allow our rules to rule over us. Even our laws need to be sanctified by the sanctifier (God's Holy Spirit). And if they are not worthy to be sanctified, they should be jettisoned.

Jesus told us he "came to seek and save the lost." (Luke 19:10) He certainly did that. But along the way, he did a few other things as well. The healing of the woman with the crippling spirit is just one example. Too many times, our penchant for doing what we think is right actually gets in the way. We become like the synagogue ruler and his cohorts. We would rather stand in Jesus' way than have him do something with which we don't agree. Our attitude becomes one of, "Lord, touch this man's life; but make sure you do it the way I want you to do it."

We are not the healer, the Savior, or the lawgiver. We are his witnesses. When the witnesses begin to lay down the law to the healer, we are running afoul of God's purposes in this world. Jesus is the Savior of all — even our humanity. Never allow the law to demean that humanity. Each of us is precious to him. We should be precious to each other as well.

We Christians like to say, "Love the sinner, hate the sin." That's okay as far as it goes, but don't let it go too far. Don't allow your hatred for someone else's sin to negate your compassion for them. Ask yourself the question we like to wear on our wrists. *WWJD* — What would Jesus do?

The answer is clear. He would love the sinner. He would have compassion for that sinner. He would eat, speak, and hang out with that sinner. Taking actions like those often ran afoul of the Jewish religious laws. Doing them rendered one unclean — disabled, if you will.

The woman with the crippling spirit was a sinner. She was in need of healing. Jesus didn't allow legalistic attitudes disable his ability or willingness to do something about her condition. When we walk with Jesus, we dare not allow our own attitudes to cripple our ability to follow in his footsteps.

Watch This!

The first verse of this chapter in Luke is fascinating all on its own. Luke indicated that Jesus was being "carefully watched." It almost sounds like a spy novel. Better yet, it sounds like Big Brother keeping an eye on unwary citizens. Jesus, of course, knew all this was happening. He warned us to be alert, and I'm sure he was vigilant as well.

As a congregation, we've gotten access to the demographics of our surrounding area. It's amazing what we know about the people we call neighbors. We are located in a rather affluent area, so it's very interesting to note the nicknames the demographers and sociologists have given the various groupings of folks that live in our immediate vicinity.

For example: The largest demographic grouping in our region is named "American Royalty" or "Power Elite." They are described as having "high aesthetic sensibilities," a "global perspective," a "drive for affluence," with a thriving "sense of well-being." The American Royalty group along with the second group makes up over 50% of the population in our region.

That second group has been labeled the "Generational Soup" or "Flourishing Families" group. They are described as being "very sociable" and "indulgent." They have a "high devotion to family" and also have a "high sense of well-being." This group has a high expectation for relevant programming.

The big question one might ask is, "How is this information attained?" The answer is primarily through spending habits. In an age when the vast majority of people use plastic for their purchases, gathering the information to make these kinds of analyses is relatively simple. For many years, the church would not do this because it was thought to be intrusive.

The business world has been using this sort of information for years. They use it to sell their product or introduce the public to some new service. It's readily obtainable on a grand scale, and they have no compunction about getting to know the habits of possible consumers.

The church finally decided, as long as it's already out there for public consumption, we may as well use it as a tool to better reach our neighbors. As it turns out, we are more "carefully watched" than ever before. Unless we're totally living "off the grid," the credit card companies have enough general information to categorize us, analyze our spending habits, see where we go, and understand what we like. We are, indeed, being carefully watched.

The church is simply taking the general information gathered by someone else and attempting to apply it for the winning of souls. The more we know about our neighbors, the better we'll be able to find ways to reach out to them. In essence, we'll make more educated attempts to touch their lives in ways that relate to who they really are.

Jesus did a similar thing. People were intently watching him. Some did so because they were looking for ways to trip him up. Others did so because they believed he was someone special — someone who could teach them or help them in some way. There were probably others who carefully watched him out of a deep sense of curiosity.

Jesus used this to his (and their) advantage. He knew they were watching him. I'm sure he had a pretty good read on why they were watching him as well. In fact, he had been invited to the home of a "prominent Pharisee." It's no secret how most of their ilk felt about Jesus. When confronted by them, he seldom held back. Among other things, he had called them hypocrites and snakes (Matthew 23:13 and v. 33). Chances are he had not been invited for a make-up session.

The setting is not only at the home of a Pharisee, but the day was the sabbath. One of the Pharisee's guests was a man with an unusual malady. This was a set-up if Jesus ever saw one. And, as scripture so aptly points out, Jesus "was being carefully watched." The guest with the "abnormal swelling of his body" (Luke 14:2) was positioned right in front of the Lord. I'm guessing the Pharisee wanted to make sure there was no way Jesus could miss the man's suffering.

Understanding the situation, Jesus asked the religious types at the gathering if it was lawful to heal on the sabbath. No one uttered a peep. Hearing no objections, Jesus healed the poor soul and "sent him on his way" (Luke 14:4). I find it interesting that the man was sent on his way was once he was healed. Had he been an important guest, the Pharisee would undoubtedly have wanted him to remain. As it was, he was a mere prop in the Pharisee's ploy to catch Jesus in a sin.

Apparently, they had all been invited to eat. After the guests arrived, Jesus noticed how people chose their places at the table. At least some of them were vying for the places of honor. The guest of honor would, according to custom, be placed at the head of the table - the closer to the guest of honor, the better the position. The host normally took the second position while the rest of the guests would fall in line from there.

So not only was Jesus being carefully observed he was doing a little observing himself. He decided to impart some truth that would become a theme throughout his public, earthly ministry. As he often did, he used a parable to get his point across.

His parable had a similar setting to the one they were in at the time. It was a wedding feast, and some of the guests were assuming places of honor. Jesus admonished them not to do this. His reasoning was that "a person more distinguished than you may have been invited" (Luke 14:8). If that happens to be the case, it will turn into an embarrassing situation for everyone — particularly for the one who tried to get the better position. Jesus points out that the host will have to ask you to move and let the more important guest take your place. Embarrassing indeed.

Jesus did not leave it at that, however. He went a step further. He gave everyone this advice: "But when you are invited, take the lowest place" (Luke 14:10). I'm not sure how that sounded to most of the guests there that day, but I'm sure at least some of them would have found it to be quite demeaning to do so. The ones who had made sure they had the better places were probably a bit miffed that he would even bring it up.

Still, Jesus wasn't finished. He added a reason for humbling oneself and taking the lowest position. He says, "When your host comes, he will say to you,

'Friend, move up to a better place.'" This sounds almost like a sneaky ploy to get publicly honored, but it would have fit right into the attitude of those trying to attain greater status for themselves. If they were humble (according to Jesus), they would have been honored by the host before all the guests — which is what they wanted in the first place.

Jesus then added his famous line in verse eleven. "For all those who exalt themselves will be humbled, and those who humble themselves will be exalted." As I mentioned before, this was one of the recurring themes throughout his ministry. Be humble and you will be exalted. Take the last place, and you will be moved up. "So the last will be first, and the first will be last" (Matthew 20:16). He continually drove that point home to his disciples (and anyone else who would listen). Being humble was obviously a big priority for him.

If all this wasn't enough, Jesus then had a word for his host. It was virtually the opposite end of the honored guest spectrum. He suggested a new guest list to the conniving Pharisee. Instead of inviting the rich and famous, his family and friends, or any other person who could add to his status, Jesus advocated for some new people. He told the man to invite the down and out, the disabled and poor, and the dregs of the earth.

I'm sure the Pharisee was beside himself upon hearing those words. He wasn't about to soil his home with such people. They would cause him to be unclean. He certainly couldn't have that. Why would this itinerant preacher even suggest such a thing?

Why indeed? According to Jesus, the answer to that question is simply this. That kind of guest list would bring blessing with it. The rich and famous could invite him back. That would be his reward. The down and outers couldn't repay his kindness. Therefore his reward would be in Heaven. As Jesus put it, "You will be repaid at the resurrection of the righteous." For Jesus, it came down to either receiving a pat on the back here on earth, or reaping riches in Heaven. It's really a no-brainer when you think about it. Regrettably, we seldom do think about it.

Still, many of us opt for the pat on the back. We look to receive our glory here and now. If we can get a leg up, a little more status, a higher position, we'll take it now. Maybe we can earn a little blessing later — after we've gained what we want in this life.

Jesus was being watched closely that day. He knew it and took advantage of it. He used the whole scenario to teach us all a few life lessons. We know the stories well. We can quote some of the verses. Unfortunately, we're also very good at forgetting what they mean.

The Lord wasn't kidding when he told us to be humble. He wasn't joking when he suggested we take the lower positions. He wasn't jiving when he pointed out that the first would be last and the last first. He keeps driving home the point, but too many of us aren't at home to hear it. We're off making a way for ourselves.

The sad thing is, we are being watched as well. We're being watched by a world that thinks we're nothing but hypocrites — Pharisaical types. Too often, we prove them to be correct. We take the best and leave nothing for others. We're on the lookout for number one without regard for numbers two through 99.

When we place ourselves first, we demonstrate to the watching world that the sayings of Christ mean nothing. We suggest to others that those words are mere platitudes to be mouthed and forgotten. We certainly aren't winning the hearts and minds of those who think the church is full of greedy and money-grabbing people.

There's another carefully watching us as well. That other is the Lord, himself. It's not that he's like some Big Brother in the sky keeping tabs every time we mess up. In fact, it's just the opposite. He's looking for opportunities to bless us, just as he told the prominent Pharisee. Sadly, those opportunities for the Lord to bless us come few and far between. It's not because we never get the chance to be there for others, it's more like we don't take the chance.

And that might be the crux of our problem. The Pharisees wouldn't invite people into their homes whom they considered to be lesser than themselves. They wouldn't take that chance. They might be considered unclean or less than sophisticated.

How many times do we pass up opportunities to invite people into our lives because we won't chance it? They don't come up to our standards or they just aren't our type. If I'm reading scripture correctly, that makes us hypocrites.

It seems to me, we should be the ones who are carefully watching. We should be watching for opportunities to touch the lives of the less fortunate. We should be looking for ways to serve our fellow human beings. We should be finding avenues to use the gifts, talents, abilities, and riches the Lord has bestowed upon us.

When we fail to do those things, we fail a watching world, we fail the Lord, and consequently, we fail ourselves. We've been given so much. We've been invited to the Lord's banquet table. As honored guests, maybe we should be looking for others to take our places. They need it just as much as we do.

Don't worry. The Lord is not going to leave us out in the cold. He's watching carefully.